WON FOR ALL

Cleveland's NBA championship

*A journey through the Cavaliers' 2015-16 season,
as told in the pages of The Plain Dealer and on cleveland.com*

THE PLAIN DEALER

Reporters/writers: Terry Pluto, Bill Livingston, Dennis Manoloff
Photographers: Charles Crow, Gus Chan, Lisa DeJong, Thomas Ondrey   **Chief photographer:** Lynn Ischay
Editor: George Rodrigue   **Assistant managing editor/sports:** Mike Starkey

Sports copy editors: Chris Ball, Keith Bracken, Greg Darroch, Tim Graham, Skip Hall, Bob Proske, Mark Spang
Illustrators: Ted Crow, Chris Morris
Sports designers: Andrea Zagata, Tony Lariccia
Sports curation lead: Bob Keim   **Copy chief:** Mike Mentrek
Publications director: Daryl Kannberg   **Assistant managing editor/visuals:** Josh Crutchmer

Book design, graphics and photo production: Josh Crutchmer

Reporters/writers: Chris Fedor, Christopher Haynes, Bud Shaw, Joe Vardon
Sports managers: David Campbell, Jamie Turner
Photographers: Joshua Gunter, John Kuntz
Vice president of content: Christopher Quinn   **President, Advance Ohio:** Tim Knight

---

This book contains content published in The Plain Dealer and on cleveland.com during the 2015-16 NBA season. Dates on stories reflect publication dates on cleveland.com.

Cover images: Front: AP Photo / Back: Thomas Ondrey | The Plain Dealer

---

Peter J. Clark, Publisher
Katherine Grigsby, Layout & Design
Special thanks to Allie Kalsow and Corey Clifton

ISBN: 978-1-940056-40-1 (PB)
ISBN: 978-1-940056-39-5 (HC)

Printed in the United States of America
KCI Sports Publishing | 3340 Whiting Avenue, Suite 5 Stevens Point, WI 54481
Phone: 1-800-697-3756 Fax: 715-344-2668
www.kcisports.com

Contents

UNFORGETTABLE

Austin Carr | *"Mr. Cavalier"*

Against all odds, the Cavaliers did it.

Cleveland Cavaliers — NBA Champions!

Sounds pretty good doesn't it? I know Cleveland fans have waited an awfully long time to utter those words, and finally, the Cavaliers are on top.

Let the celebration begin!

It's my honor to write the foreword for a book chronicling such a historic season. It's not easy winning in the NBA. The Cavs have been close before, but for whatever reason weren't able to get over the hump. Until now. This was a championship team that had been months in the making. Head coach Tyronn Lue had a clear vision when he was brought on board: play to the strengths of LeBron James, Kyrie Irving, Kevin Love and the rest of this talented group.

Mission accomplished.

In the following pages, the Plain Dealer and cleveland.com proudly bring you on a trip down memory lane of this championship season that came to its jubilant conclusion in Game 7 in Oakland. Won For All provides Cavs fans the best view in the house of all the ups and downs of the season and gives you an inside look at the incredible comeback in the NBA Finals against a very talented Golden State Warriors team.

Celebrate this season Cavs fans, and save this book to revisit the Cavaliers' magical moments and unforgettable team — both stars and role players — who rewarded your faith in the Wine & Gold with our first ever NBA championship.

Congratulation Cavaliers! Let's do it again soon.

Mr. Cavalier,

Austin Carr

LeBron James embraces his two boys, LeBron Jr. and Bryce, after winning the championship.

GUS CHAN | THE PLAIN DEALER

BELIEVE IT!

TERRY PLUTO | *The Plain Dealer*
June 20, 2016

It's over. ¶ OK, Cleveland sports fans, take a deep breath, then say those two words — It's over. ¶ A major sports championship is yours for the first time since the 1964 Browns. ¶ Thank you, Cavaliers. ¶ Thank you, LeBron James. ¶ Thank you for the stunning 93-89 victory over the Golden State Warriors at Oracle Arena. ¶ Thank you for not only delivering an NBA title, but making history ... defying the odds ... confounding the critics. ¶ The Cavs didn't just win their first NBA title, they won in a fashion the NBA has never seen before. Down, 3-1, and facing elimination, they came back to win the seven-game series. ¶ That's a first. ¶ Going on the road to win a Game 7 in the Finals. That hasn't been done since 1978. ¶ The Cavs didn't just win, they upset the defending NBA champions. They beat a team that won an NBA record 73 games during the regular season. ¶ They turned the basketball world upside down — and came out on top! ¶ Fifty-two years of tears, heartache and frustration are over.

Cavaliers coach Tyronn Lue embraces general manager David Griffin after winning the title.

GUS CHAN | THE PLAIN DEALER

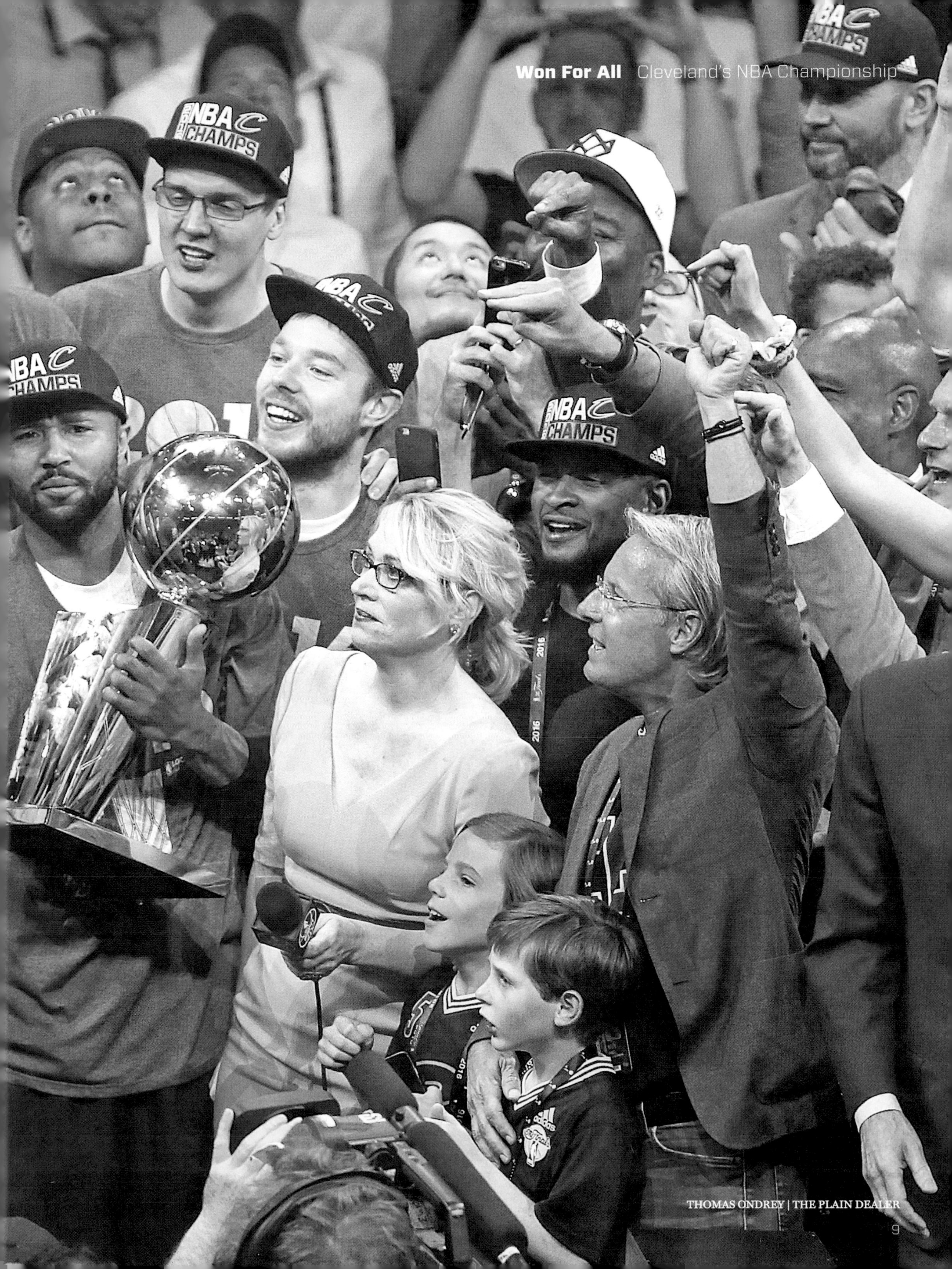

THOMAS ONDREY | THE PLAIN DEALER

FIRST, A COMING TOGETHER

CHRIS HAYNES | *Cleveland.com*
October 28, 2015

LeBron James, Cleveland Cavaliers held a team meeting with a clear message: Get down to business, now

As the start of the regular season grew closer, LeBron James' patience grew thin.

The last few weeks, the captain hasn't been happy with the team's frame of mind and has used his voice to send a message that pursuing a championship requires a businesslike mindset from the start.

James wasn't the only one who noticed something didn't feel right about the team's demeanor. Other players saw it too, prompting a team meeting before they took off for an exhibition game at Toronto on Oct. 17.

"[We were] just making sure everybody is doing the right thing and having the right goals in their heads," the Cavs' Sasha Kaun said of that meeting.

Players, I'm told, spoke up about not liking what some considered to be a increasingly loose, frolicsome atmosphere. James, I'm told, chimed in on the need to straighten up. Guidelines were given and a renewed commitment was established.

The weight of the world is on James' shoulders. He knows how much a championship would mean to the city of Cleveland. The Cavaliers may have the talent and depth to contend, but unless they approach the season the right way, the amount of quality players won't mean a thing.

"All I care about is raising banners," James said. "Nothing else. That's what I'm here for."

James' mood has been somber. He's setting the tone.

The Cavaliers have a vast collection of personalities and backgrounds. They can be an entertaining bunch, but that's not the perception James and other players want on a regular basis.

The Cavs have a three-month window to find themselves and get by without Kyrie Irving and Iman Shumpert.

After that, James isn't naive to think they'll be able to just flip the switch and get serious once everybody is healthy. He has informed his team that it's time to buckle down, now.

"Yeah, you can see it," James said. "You can also tell if guys are messing around a little too much. Me as a leader, I'm able to gauge that and see where our minds are at."

The championship quest is now and the memo was crystal clear: It's time to get down to business.

LeBron James and then-Cavs assistant Tyronn Lue, during a preseason game against Dallas. JOSHUA GUNTER | CLEVELAND.COM

Warriors 89, Cavaliers 83

FAMILIAR DISAPPOINTMENT

CHRIS HAYNES | *Cleveland.com*
December 25, 2015

In NBA Finals rematch, Golden State defeats Cavs on Christmas Day

OAKLAND, Calif. — The anticipation, the suspense, the build-up to Friday's Christmas Day Finals rematch between the Cleveland Cavaliers and Golden State Warriors didn't disappoint.

It was a back and forth affair. The atmosphere was rowdy. Matthew Dellavedova was booed viciously upon entering the game midway in the first quarter. There's no love lost.

It had the feeling of an extension of their series in June and unfortunately for the Cavaliers, it garnered the same result: the Warriors coming away on top at Oracle Arena.

Draymond Green flirted with a triple-double by registering 22 points, 15 rebounds and seven assists for Golden State (28-1). Stephen Curry dropped 19 points, Klay Thompson put in 18 points and Shaun Livingston provided 16.

Judging by the players, every wasted possession looked as if it was a colossal failure.

"I think it's good for the NBA," Warriors interim coach Luke Walton said of the fan interest in watching these two teams face off. "I wouldn't call it a rivalry, but we are linked. We had a really competitive NBA Finals last year, and they're one of the best teams in the East and we're one of the best teams in the West."

SATURDAY, DECEMBER 26, 2015

Sports

Warriors 89, Cavaliers 83

Clink, clank, clunk

By game's end, LeBron James had scored 25 points, with nine rebounds and two blocks. But he hit only 10-of-26 attempts and missed two key free throws at the end of game.

MARCIO JOSE SANCHEZ | ASSOCIATED PRESS

Cavaliers shoot only 32 percent, Big 3 are 19-of-57 in Finals rematch

CHRIS HAYNES | chaynes@cleveland.com

OAKLAND, CALIF. — The Cavaliers wanted a shot at redemption with the champions so badly, but couldn't make a shot to get the job done Friday night. ¶ "I think it was heavy on all of our minds," Cavs guard J.R. Smith said of the buildup to the game. "I think we put too much pressure on ourselves to want to go out there and play well." ¶ The ultimate holiday achievement for the Cavaliers would have been the successful delivery of a second loss into the Christmas stockings of the Golden State Warriors. ¶ Instead, the Warriors weren't in the mood for receiving. They were in the giving spirit. In an NBA Finals rematch on Christmas Day the Warriors handed the Cavaliers a loss, 89-83 at Oracle Arena. ¶ For some reason, the Cavaliers weren't in the giving spirit because they refused to share the wealth. They gave the Warriors' defense the day off by choosing to play isolation basketball, rather than swinging it around for easier scoring opportunities.

SEE CAVALIERS | B4

Next for Cavs vs. Trail Blazers | 10 p.m. today | Moda Center, Portland, Oregon | TV: FSO | Radio: WTAM AM/1100, WMMS FM/100.7

HUMBLED AGAIN

DENNIS MANOLOFF | *The Plain Dealer*
January 18, 2016

S tephen Curry scored 35 and posted a +34 in 28 minutes as the Golden State Warriors destroyed the Cleveland Cavaliers, 132-98, Monday night at The Q. LeBron James scored 16 for the Cavs.

So much for that: The Cavs (28-11 overall, 15-2 at home) were coming off a 5-1 trip that ended with a decisive victory in Houston on Friday night.

The Warriors (38-4 overall, 19-4 on the road) were coming off a loss in Detroit on Saturday.

One-sided: The Warriors have won five straight against the Cavs. They won the last three games of the 2015 NBA Finals and swept the season series.

On Christmas Day in Oakland, the Warriors won a highly competitive game, 89-83.

Yikes: On Monday, Golden State was awesome and the Cavs were absolutely terrible. A lot of what the Warriors did made the Cavs terrible.

No matter what Cavs personnel says, this loss was so ugly that it undoubtedly will linger to some degree for the remainder of the season and playoffs.

Globetrotters vs. Generals: The Warriors (38-4) dominated virtually from the opening tip.

Curry's Warriors humiliate James and the Cavaliers at The Q

Golden State's Stephen Curry watches the clock tick down on the Warriors' convincing win. JOHN KUNTZ | CLEVELAND.COM

SUDDENLY, A SHAKEUP AT THE TOP

CHRIS FEDOR | *Cleveland.com*
January 22, 2016

Sitting atop the Eastern Conference at 30-11, the Cavaliers fire head coach David Blatt

Four days following the Cleveland Cavaliers' worst loss of the season, against the Golden State Warriors, the team fired head coach David Blatt. ¶ Tyronn Lue, Blatt's top assistant, was elevated as head coach effective immediately. The Cavs will host the Chicago Bulls Saturday night at Quicken Loans Arena. ¶ Blatt helped lead the Cavaliers to the NBA Finals in his first season, losing to the Warriors, 4-2. An expected title contender once again this season, the Cavaliers are 30-11, the top seed in the Eastern Conference, and have won 11 of the last 13 games. However, the two losses have come against the league's elite, Golden State and San Antonio. ¶ Blatt, one of the most decorated coaches in European basketball history before coming to the NBA, finishes his Cleveland tenure with a regular season record of 83-40. ¶ "I am very grateful to have had the opportunity to serve as the Head Coach of the Cleveland Cavaliers," Blatt wrote in a statement released by Priority Sports and Entertainment on Friday. "I'd like to thank Dan Gilbert and David Griffin for giving me this opportunity and am honored to have worked with an amazing group of players from LeBron James, Kyrie Irving and Kevin Love through our entire roster. ¶ "I'd also like to express my extreme gratitude to my coaching staff. I am indebted to them for their professionalism hard work, loyalty and friendship. I am proud of what we have accomplished since I have been the Head Coach and wish the Cavaliers nothing but the best this season and beyond."

David Blatt on the sidelines in his final game as Cavs' coach, a 115-102 win over the Clippers. CHUCK CROW | THE PLAIN DEALER

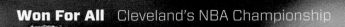

CHRIS MORRIS
THE PLAIN DEALER

Lue named coach

SEASON RESTS ON NEW SHOULDERS

BILL LIVINGSTON | *The Plain Dealer*
January 22, 2016

Breakup of Blatt and Cavs leaves new coach little time to pick up the pieces

The body language of estranged player and embattled coach hinted of a break-up for a long time.

And thus did King LeBron and his Court, the Cavaliers' supporting players, finally send David Blatt to the unemployment line.

In the NBA Finals, LeBron James would look off into the crowd during timeouts, blatantly ignoring his coach, sometimes vetoing a play and drawing up his own. The distracted, exasperated gaze into the distance was an old James' tactic in the last days for Mike Brown in 2010.

It took five straight seasons of Brown's primitive offense and of a front office supplying mismatched parts to make him leave.

Blatt, however, did not have even Brown's pedigree as an NBA assistant. He instead was a very successful European coach who was hired to rebuild a team, one that James' return alone was supposed to turn from chumps to champs.

At Friday's news conference, general manager David Griffin spoke of a "disconnect" in the locker room between players and coach. However, 30-11, the Cavs' record, is a 60-win season in the making.

Griffin said the firing was his call, but it has that old, modern athlete stench of the inmates running the asylum. Blatt was dumped even after injuries knocked Kevin Love and Kyrie Irving out of most of the playoffs in the first case and most of the Finals in the second.

Because James is James, the most extravagantly gifted player on the floor in almost every game he has ever played, it will all ultimately circle back to him. He is Our Restored Civic Treasure again; after he left, he was Not Quite Art Modell; and now he is coming off as LeBron II, succeeding himself on the throne in his second term here because no one else was worthy.

As an encouraging historical precedent, Magic Johnson fired coach Paul Westhead after only 11 games in the 1981-82 season.

The Lakers had also been dethroned in the first round of the previous year's playoffs by Houston, a team with a losing record. The Lakers, by the way, went on to win the championship that season under Pat Riley, then a former assistant coach who landed in his first head coaching job.

Riley was team president in Miami when James won two championships in four years. Riley commanded all players' respect with his record. Maybe Lue will too, although the record part is comparatively thin.

If so, that might be a first for a Cavs coach with James, but Lue had better work on it.

'A KICK IN THE REAR END'

CHRIS FEDOR | *Cleveland.com*
January 29, 2016

James is only Cav honored while Lue coaches All-Star Game in place of Blatt

The Cavaliers, known for their formidable Big Three, will be represented by a Big One in Toronto for the 2016 NBA All-Star Game.

LeBron James, voted a starter by the fans, was the only player selected from the Eastern Conference's top seed, as Kyrie Irving and Kevin Love were left out.

"It's definitely a kick in the rear end for our team for sure, knowing all the work we put into it, and knowing the two other guys," James said prior to Friday morning's shootaround. "You know, Kyrie's games being limited like that I figured the coaches wouldn't give him the nod, but you know he's an All-Star. And then with Kev, I think Kev has played great basketball for the first half of the season."

But the Cavaliers tried to make the case for Love. It didn't work.

"I just thought, in this league it's always been about winning and winning has always been rewarded," said Tyronn Lue, who will be coaching the East's All-Star squad. "Being No. 1 in the East and Kevin being one of four guys in the NBA to average a double-double on a winning team, I've just never seen being a first-place team and getting one guy in."

In the Cavs' final game before the All-Star break, they defeated the Lakers 120-111 in Kobe Bryant's final game in Cleveland. JOSHUA GUNTER | CLEVELAND.COM

Date	Opponent	W/L	Score	Record	Date	Opponent	W/L	Score	Record
Oct 27, 2015	@ Chicago Bulls	L	95-97	0 - 1	Jan 23, 2016	vs. Chicago Bulls	L	83-96	30 - 12
Oct 28, 2015	@ Memphis Grizzlies	W	106-76	1 - 1	Jan 25, 2016	vs. Minnesota Timberwolves	W	114-107	31 - 12
Oct 30, 2015	vs. Miami Heat	W	102-92	2 - 1	Jan 27, 2016	vs. Phoenix Suns	W	115-93	32 - 12
Nov 02, 2015	@ Philadelphia 76ers	W	107-100	3 - 1	Jan 29, 2016	@ Detroit Pistons	W	114-106	33 - 12
Nov 04, 2015	vs. New York Knicks	W	96-86	4 - 1	Jan 30, 2016	vs. San Antonio Spurs	W	117-103	34 - 12
Nov 06, 2015	vs. Philadelphia 76ers	W	108-102	5 - 1	Feb 01, 2016	@ Indiana Pacers	W (OT)	111-106	35 - 12
Nov 08, 2015	vs. Indiana Pacers	W	101-97	6 - 1	Feb 03, 2016	@ Charlotte Hornets	L	97-106	35 - 13
Nov 10, 2015	vs. Utah Jazz	W	118-114	7 - 1	Feb 05, 2016	vs. Boston Celtics	L	103-104	35 - 14
Nov 13, 2015	@ New York Knicks	W	90-84	8 - 1	Feb 06, 2016	vs. New Orleans Pelicans	W	99-84	36 - 14
Nov 14, 2015	@ Milwaukee Bucks	L (OT)	105-108	8 - 2	Feb 08, 2016	vs. Sacramento Kings	W	120-100	37 - 14
Nov 17, 2015	@ Detroit Pistons	L	99-104	8 - 3	Feb 10, 2016	vs. Los Angeles Lakers	W	120-111	38 - 14
Nov 19, 2015	vs. Milwaukee Bucks	W	115-100	9 - 3	Feb 18, 2016	vs. Chicago Bulls	W	106-95	39 - 14
Nov 21, 2015	vs. Atlanta Hawks	W	109-97	10 - 3	Feb 21, 2016	@ Oklahoma City Thunder	W	115-92	40 - 14
Nov 23, 2015	vs. Orlando Magic	W	117-103	11 - 3	Feb 22, 2016	vs. Detroit Pistons	L	88-96	40 - 15
Nov 25, 2015	@ Toronto Raptors	L	99-103	11 - 4	Feb 24, 2016	vs. Charlotte Hornets	W	114-103	41 - 15
Nov 27, 2015	@ Charlotte Hornets	W	95-90	12 - 4	Feb 26, 2016	@ Toronto Raptors	L	97-99	41 - 16
Nov 28, 2015	vs. Brooklyn Nets	W	90-88	13 - 4	Feb 28, 2016	@ Washington Wizards	L	99-113	41 - 17
Dec 01, 2015	vs. Washington Wizards	L	85-97	13 - 5	Feb 29, 2016	vs. Indiana Pacers	W	100-96	42 - 17
Dec 04, 2015	@ New Orleans Pelicans	L (OT)	108-114	13 - 6	Mar 04, 2016	vs. Washington Wizards	W	108-83	43 - 17
Dec 05, 2015	@ Miami Heat	L	84-99	13 - 7	Mar 05, 2016	vs. Boston Celtics	W	120-103	44 - 17
Dec 08, 2015	vs. Portland Trail Blazers	W	105-100	14 - 7	Mar 07, 2016	vs. Memphis Grizzlies	L	103-106	44 - 18
Dec 11, 2015	@ Orlando Magic	W	111-76	15 - 7	Mar 09, 2016	@ Sacramento Kings	W	120-111	45 - 18
Dec 15, 2015	@ Boston Celtics	W	89-77	16 - 7	Mar 10, 2016	@ Los Angeles Lakers	W	120-108	46 - 18
Dec 17, 2015	vs. Oklahoma City Thunder	W	104-100	17 - 7	Mar 13, 2016	@ Los Angeles Clippers	W	114-90	47 - 18
Dec 20, 2015	vs. Philadelphia 76ers	W	108-86	18 - 7	Mar 14, 2016	@ Utah Jazz	L	85-94	47 - 19
Dec 23, 2015	vs. New York Knicks	W	91-84	19 - 7	Mar 16, 2016	vs. Dallas Mavericks	W	99-98	48 - 19
Dec 25, 2015	@ Golden State Warriors	L	83-89	19 - 8	Mar 18, 2016	@ Orlando Magic	W	109-103	49 - 19
Dec 26, 2015	@ Portland Trail Blazers	L	76-105	19 - 9	Mar 19, 2016	@ Miami Heat	L	101-122	49 - 20
Dec 28, 2015	@ Phoenix Suns	W	101-97	20 - 9	Mar 21, 2016	vs. Denver Nuggets	W	124-91	50 - 20
Dec 29, 2015	@ Denver Nuggets	W	93-87	21 - 9	Mar 23, 2016	vs. Milwaukee Bucks	W	113-104	51 - 20
Jan 02, 2016	vs. Orlando Magic	W	104-79	22 - 9	Mar 24, 2016	@ Brooklyn Nets	L	95-104	51 - 21
Jan 04, 2016	vs. Toronto Raptors	W	122-100	23 - 9	Mar 26, 2016	@ New York Knicks	W	107-93	52 - 21
Jan 06, 2016	@ Washington Wizards	W	121-115	24 - 9	Mar 29, 2016	vs. Houston Rockets	L	100-106	52 - 22
Jan 08, 2016	@ Minnesota Timberwolves	W	125-99	25 - 9	Mar 31, 2016	vs. Brooklyn Nets	W	107-87	53 - 22
Jan 10, 2016	@ Philadelphia 76ers	W	95-85	26 - 9	Apr 01, 2016	@ Atlanta Hawks	W (OT)	110-108	54 - 22
Jan 12, 2016	@ Dallas Mavericks	W (OT)	110-107	27 - 9	Apr 03, 2016	vs. Charlotte Hornets	W	112-103	55 - 22
Jan 14, 2016	@ San Antonio Spurs	L	95-99	27 - 10	Apr 05, 2016	@ Milwaukee Bucks	W	109-80	56 - 22
Jan 15, 2016	@ Houston Rockets	W	91-77	28 - 10	Apr 06, 2016	@ Indiana Pacers	L	109-123	56 - 23
Jan 18, 2016	vs. Golden State Warriors	L	98-132	28 - 11	Apr 09, 2016	@ Chicago Bulls	L	102-105	56 - 24
Jan 20, 2016	@ Brooklyn Nets	W	91-78	29 - 11	Apr 11, 2016	vs. Atlanta Hawks	W	109-94	57 - 24
Jan 21, 2016	vs. Los Angeles Clippers	W	115-102	30 - 11	Apr 13, 2016	vs. Detroit Pistons	L (OT)	110-112	57 - 25

LeBron James dunks against the Hawks in a 109-94 win on April 11 that clinched top seed in the Eastern Conference. GUS CHAN | THE PLAIN DEALER

TOP SEED

DENNIS MANOLOFF | *The Plain Dealer*
April 11, 2016

Kyrie Irving scored 35 and LeBron James 34 (in three quarters) as the Cleveland Cavaliers handled the Atlanta Hawks, 109-94, Monday night at The Q. The Cavs clinched the No. 1 seed in the Eastern Conference.
    As it should be: Rebounding from a stinker against the Bulls in Chicago, the Cavs played like a top seed in improving to 57-24. They did so without rotation guard Iman Shumpert (knee).
The Hawks, No. 3 in the East, slipped to 48-33.

Accepting the challenge: The Cavs -- specifically, the starters -- had plenty of incentive to make Monday's game the last meaningful one of the regular season. Now, when the 82nd game is played Wednesday against Detroit at The Q, Cavs coach Tyronn Lue can rest his best with a clear mind because the top seed has been secured.

The Hawks also were highly motivated, in part because the third seed behind Cleveland and Toronto had not been clinched. They also were sick of losing to the Cavs; the streak was six overall, including being swept in the 2015 Eastern Conference Final and dropping the first two meetings this season.

So the Hawks, who were only missing injured center Tiago Splitter, took the court with something to prove.

The Hawks no doubt thought the six-game losing streak was traceable to having been pushed around. The Cavs don't out-muscle many teams, but the Hawks have been a relatively easy mark.

From the opening tip, the Hawks were as physical as they could be -- and played well. Kent Bazemore, alone, made it 8-0. Then it was 10-0. LeBron stopped the run with a dunk with 9:09 left in the first quarter.

As of 4:05 remaining in the first, Atlanta led, 20-10. The Cavs chipped away and trailed, 26-22, by the end of the quarter. They controlled play for the vast majority of minutes the rest of the way, including a combined 68-49 advantage over the second and third quarters.

LeBron wrapped another terrific regular season, his 13th. Warriors guard Steph Curry will be voted MVP and will have earned it, but this reality shouldn't diminish what LeBron accomplished. King would have been MVP if not for the remarkable, record-setting seasons of Curry and the Warriors.

Irving, James fantastic as Cavaliers dispose of Hawks to clinch No. 1 in Eastern Conference

Season totals	GP	GS	MIN	FGM	FGA	FG%	3PM	3PA	3P%	FTM	FTA	FT%	OR	DR	REB	AST	STL	BLK	TO	PF	PTS
Jared Cunningham	40	3	355	32	91	0.352	10	32	0.313	30	48	0.625	3	26	29	19	12	2	18	37	104
Matthew Dellavedova	76	14	1867	207	511	0.405	98	239	0.410	57	66	0.864	33	129	162	337	44	9	116	178	569
Channing Frye	26	3	446	71	161	0.441	43	114	0.377	11	14	0.786	12	81	93	26	8	8	13	56	196
Joe Harris	5	0	15	1	4	0.250	1	4	0.250	0	0	0.000	0	3	3	2	0	0	1	1	3
Kyrie Irving	53	53	1667	394	879	0.448	84	262	0.321	169	191	0.885	44	113	157	250	56	18	124	107	1041
LeBron James	76	76	2709	737	1416	0.520	87	282	0.309	359	491	0.731	111	454	565	514	104	49	249	143	1920
Richard Jefferson	74	5	1326	143	312	0.458	66	173	0.382	58	87	0.667	15	113	128	59	33	14	43	129	410
Dahntay Jones	1	0	42	6	14	0.429	1	2	0.500	0	0	0.000	1	4	5	2	1	2	0	6	13
James Jones	48	0	463	58	142	0.408	41	104	0.394	21	26	0.808	8	42	50	11	11	10	13	50	178
Sasha Kaun	25	0	95	9	17	0.529	0	0	0.000	5	11	0.455	12	14	26	3	4	5	7	21	23
Kevin Love	77	77	2424	409	977	0.419	158	439	0.360	258	314	0.822	149	613	762	185	58	41	142	159	1234
Jordan McRae	15	1	113	23	52	0.442	7	11	0.636	9	13	0.692	2	10	12	15	0	1	9	10	62
Timofey Mozgov	76	48	1326	203	359	0.565	1	7	0.143	68	95	0.716	110	227	337	33	22	57	71	159	475
Iman Shumpert	54	5	1316	114	305	0.374	43	146	0.295	40	51	0.784	32	171	203	92	54	19	57	119	311
JR Smith	77	77	2362	353	850	0.415	204	510	0.400	45	71	0.634	43	174	217	130	81	21	59	204	955
Tristan Thompson	82	34	2269	247	420	0.588	0	0	0.000	149	242	0.616	268	470	738	62	38	51	61	202	643
Anderson Varejao	31	0	310	32	76	0.421	0	1	0.000	16	21	0.762	24	67	91	20	11	5	16	35	80
Mo Williams	41	14	748	132	302	0.437	36	102	0.353	38	42	0.905	6	66	72	98	14	5	57	60	338
Team	82	19855	3171	6888	0.460	880	2428	0.362	1333	1783	0.748	873	2777	3650	1861	551	317	1114	1666	8555	
Opponents	82	19855	3019	6736	0.448	647	1862	0.347	1378	1855	0.743	760	2604	3364	1756	590	362	1092	1690	8063	

**Members of The Q Spirit Squad greet fans during Cavs Fan Fest at Gateway Plaza before
Cleveland's first playoff game on April 17.** LISA DEJONG | THE PLAIN DEALER

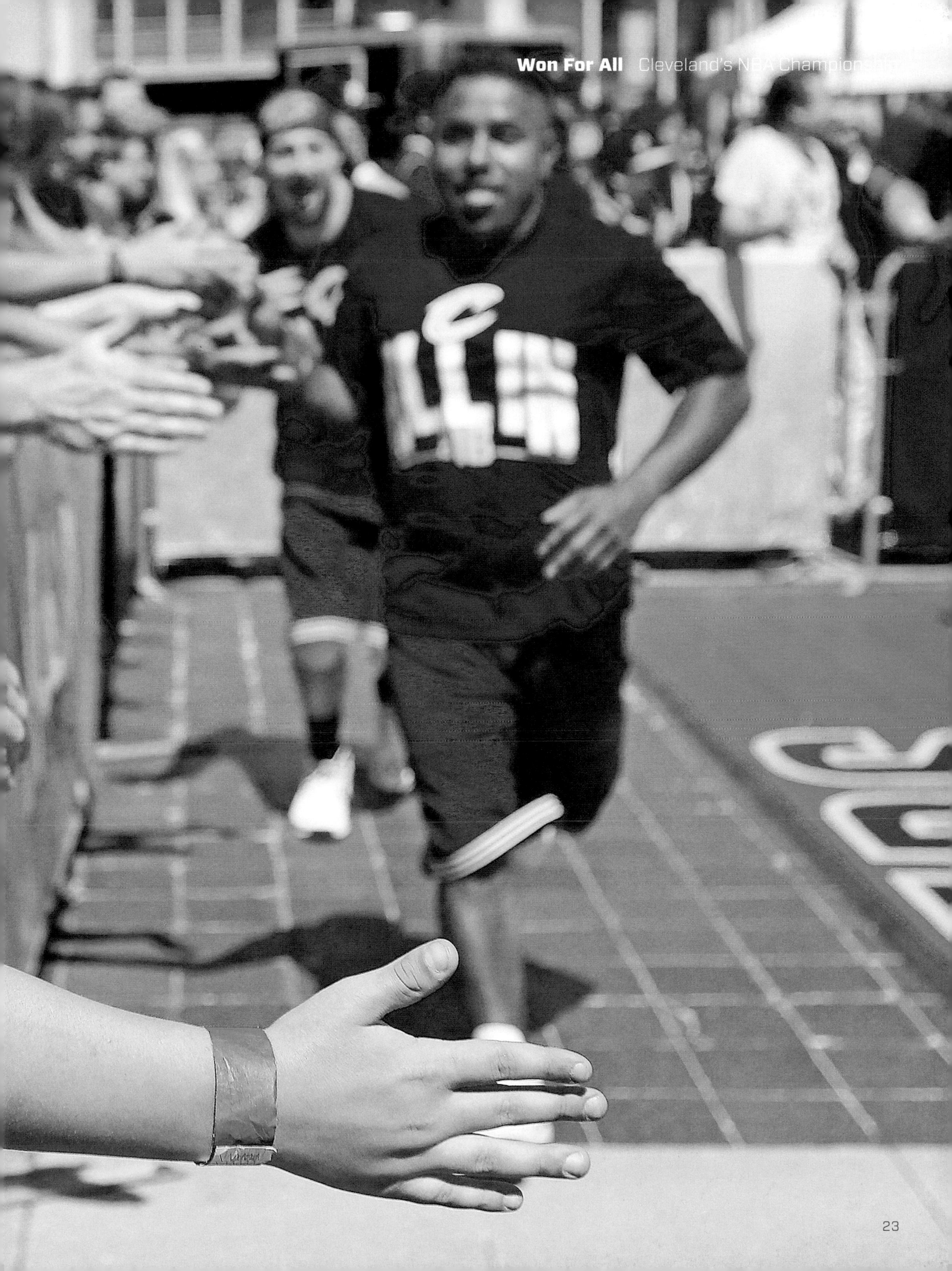

Arena

THE PLAIN DEALER

SATURDAY, APRIL 16, 2016
NBA PLAYOFFS PREVIEW
SECTION C | 8 PAGES

CLE vs DET

SOLITARY FOCUS

LeBron James is distraction-free and dialed in.
If the Cavs follow his lead, a title run awaits.

FIRST ROUND CAVALIERS VS. PISTONS

ILLUSTRATION BY TED CROW
THE PLAIN DEALER

PLAYOFFS BRING A NEW FOCUS FOR CAVALIERS

JOE VARDON | *cleveland.com*
April 16, 2016

I
f the Pistons win a game against the Cavaliers in this Eastern Conference first-round series, it's a major story.

Why? Because LeBron James doesn't lose first-round games.

James' teams have not lost a single opening-round contest since May 6, 2012, when the Miami Heat fell to the New York Knicks in Game 4 and failed to complete the sweep.

He's won the last 13, including the four the Cavs took uninterrupted from Boston to open last year's playoffs.

James is of course a two-time champion and is gunning for his sixth consecutive Finals – something that hasn't been done since the Boston Celtics in the 1960s.

But his first-round dominance over 10 previous playoff runs is something to behold. James has never lost an opening series. Michael Jordan's Bulls team lost three times in the first round, as did Larry Bird's Celtics. Kobe Bryant and Magic Johnson each lost twice in the first round. Shaquille O'Neal had ample first-round series losses. Stephen Curry and the Warriors didn't make it out of the first round once.

So, you might say if the No. 8 Pistons somehow were to bounce the No. 1 seed Cavs from the tournament, it would be perhaps the biggest upset in NBA playoff history.

But you can say that about any team facing a James-led squad in the first round.

"Just his greatness. He's a winner and has always been a winner and he's always been able to lead his team, like you said, to the playoffs," Cavs coach Tyronn Lue said Saturday, when asked about James' first-round streak. "What is it, five straight NBA Finals? OI I mean, that's remarkable. With LeBron, it's a credit to him and how hard he has worked and like you said, putting his team on his back and being able to win every year in the playoffs."

This isn't to say the Cavs are disrespecting the Pistons entering the series. To a man, Cleveland's coaches and players have praised Detroit coach Stan Van Gundy, big man Andre Drummond, point guard Reggie Jackson, and so on. At 44 wins, these Pistons are in fact the best team on paper that James has faced in the first round in many years.

For what it's worth, the Pistons beat Cleveland three times this season, though one of those was the regular-season finale Wednesday, when neither team played any of its starters.

James didn't speak to reporters Saturday. On Friday he said he expected a "a very good series."

History tells us that's not what's in the cards.

Why even one win for the Pistons over LeBron James and the Cavaliers would be a major upset

LeBron James drives to the hoop in Game 1 against Detroit.

SLEEPING GIANT AWAKENS

CHRIS HAYNES | *cleveland.com*
April 17, 2016

With Game 1 of the first-round series against Detroit in the books, the Cleveland Cavaliers finally have a reason to wake up from their three-week hibernation.

Those last 25 days of the regular season consisted of players essentially sleepwalking through the schedule. They were bored out of their minds, as one person close to the team so eloquently described it. After that 122-101 loss in Miami on March 19, there were no more marquee games on the docket and really nothing to play for.

The Toronto Raptors weren't a serious threat to overtake them as the Eastern Conference's No. 1 seed.

Cleveland was even able to rest guys here and there without losing ground. The coaching staff along with LeBron James repeatedly stressed to the team the importance of respecting the process and maintaining a high level of intensity.

On Sunday, Detroit used the first 3 ½ quarters to make a barrage of 3-pointers that gave them a seven-point lead with about 6 minutes to play. That's when Cleveland heard the alarm clock and removed its sleeping masks.

For so long, they haven't had to.

Cavs are out of hibernation — and the Pistons are in trouble

PISTONS			FIELD GOALS			+/-	REBOUNDS			AST	PF	ST	TO	BS	BA	PTS
	POS	MIN	FG-A	3P-A	FT-A		OFF	DEF	TOT							
T. Harris	F	39:52	4-11	1-4	0-0	-4	1	9	10	2	1	2	3	1	3	9
M. Morris	F	39:41	6-14	3-7	5-6	-7	1	1	2	5	4	1	1	0	0	20
A. Drummond	C	36:32	6-14	0-1	1-2	-4	3	8	11	0	3	0	0	1	0	13
K. Caldwell-Pope	G	38:22	7-14	4-8	3-4	-2	0	2	2	3	2	0	0	0	0	21
R. Jackson	G	33:41	7-12	2-4	1-1	-11	0	2	2	7	3	1	3	0	1	17
S. Johnson		16:27	3-4	3-3	0-0	+1	0	8	8	0	4	0	0	0	0	9
S. Blake		14:19	0-0	0-0	1-2	+6	0	2	2	6	2	0	3	0	0	1
R. Bullock		09:38	3-3	2-2	0-0	-3	0	0	0	1	2	0	0	0	0	8
A. Baynes		11:28	1-1	0-0	1-1	-1	0	0	0	0	0	0	0	0	0	3
J. Anthony		DNP - COACH'S DECISION														
S. Dinwiddie		DNP - COACH'S DECISION														
J. Meeks		DNP - COACH'S DECISION														
A. Tolliver		DNP - COACH'S DECISION														
Total		240	37-73	15-29	12-16		5	32	37	24	21	4	10	2	4	101

TEAM REBS: 6   TOTAL TO: 12

CAVALIERS			FIELD GOALS			+/-	REBOUNDS			AST	PF	ST	TO	BS	BA	PTS
	POS	MIN	FG-A	3P-A	FT-A		OFF	DEF	TOT							
L. James	F	40:51	9-17	0-3	4-4	+18	1	5	6	11	3	2	1	2	0	22
K. Love	F	38:19	10-22	4-8	4-5	+12	3	10	13	1	2	1	2	0	2	28
T. Thompson	C	30:22	1-1	0-0	0-0	+3	4	2	6	2	2	0	0	0	0	2
J. Smith	G	35:25	3-9	2-7	1-2	+3	1	2	3	3	1	0	0	0	0	9
K. Irving	G	37:32	10-245-10	6-8	0		2	3	5	6	2	2	1	1	0	31
M. Dellavedova		19:19	3-8	0-4	1-2	-1	0	2	2	1	3	0	0	0	0	7
I. Shumpert		21:39	1-2	0-1	0-0	-4	1	3	4	0	2	0	0	0	0	2
R. Jefferson		11:59	2-4	1-2	0-0	-1	0	1	1	1	2	0	0	0	0	5
T. Mozgov		04:34	0-1	0-0	0-0	-5	0	0	0	0	1	0	1	0	0	0
C. Frye		DNP - COACH'S DECISION														
D. Jones		DNP - COACH'S DECISION														
J. Jones		DNP - COACH'S DECISION														
J. McRae		DNP - COACH'S DECISION														
Total		240	39-88	12-35	16-21		12	28	40	25	18	7	4	4	2	106

TEAM REBS: 11   TOTAL TO: 5

J.R. Smith
takes a
3-pointer in
Game 2.
JOSHUA GUNTER
CLEVELAND.COM

Cavaliers 107, Pistons 90 Game 2

A TASTE OF WHAT'S TO COME

CHRIS HAYNES | *cleveland.com*
April 20, 2016

Cavaliers tie 3-point record, take 2-0 series lead with 107-90 victory

On Sunday it took the Cleveland Cavaliers three and a half quarters before they woke up and jumped on the Detroit Pistons.

Progress is being made.

This time around on Wednesday evening at The Q, it took them two and a half quarters to put their imprint on the game. A 16-2 run by the reigning Eastern Conference champs in the middle of the third quarter was the difference-maker. It provided enough breathing space that ultimately led to the Cavaliers going up 2-0 with a 107-90 victory in this opening-round playoff series.

LeBron James registered 27 points and six rebounds. Kyrie Irving included 22 points and four assists. J.R. Smith scored 21 points -- all on seven triples.

The Cavaliers hit 20 three-pointers out of 38 attempts, tying an NBA playoff record most recently achieved by the 2015 Warriors. They were on fire.

Before Cleveland made its run, Detroit carried a 10-point lead at one point in the first half. The Pistons are a young, confident, resilient bunch.

The Cavaliers' first lead didn't come until three minutes into the second quarter.

THE PLAIN DEALER

(newspaper front page reproduction)

ROYAL TREATMENT
Cavaliers swamp the Pistons with 20 3-pointers and take a 2-0 lead

---

PISTONS	POS	MIN	FG-A	3P-A	FT-A	+/-	OFF	DEF	TOT	AST	PF	ST	TO	BS	BA	PTS
T. Harris	F	32:52	3-11	0-1	7-8	+2	3	5	8	4	5	0	1	1	0	13
M. Morris	F	34:06	2-10	1-5	6-6	+3	1	6	7	2	5	1	2	0	0	11
A. Drummond	C	36:24	8-13	0-0	4-16	-4	5	2	7	0	2	1	3	1	0	20
K. Caldwell-Pope	G	37:12	5-12	2-6	1-2	-8	0	8	8	2	2	1	1	0	1	13
R. Jackson	G	36:48	7-14	0-0	0-0	+6	2	2	4	6	3	3	1	1	0	14
S. Johnson		21:41	4-7	1-2	0-0	-20	0	2	2	0	1	0	2	0	0	9
S. Blake		09:31	0-2	0-1	0-0	-20	0	0	0	1	0	0	2	0	0	0
A. Baynes		06:25	1-3	0-0	0-0	-9	0	1	1	0	0	0	0	0	1	2
R. Bullock		12:18	2-3	0-1	0-0	-14	0	2	2	0	1	0	0	0	0	4
A. Tolliver		09:21	0-1	0-1	0-0	-15	0	1	1	0	0	0	0	0	0	0
J. Meeks		01:41	1-1	0-0	0-0	-3	0	0	0	0	0	0	0	0	0	2
S. Dinwiddie		01:41	1-1	0-0	0-0	-3	0	0	0	1	0	0	0	0	0	2
J. Anthony	DNP - COACH'S DECISION															
Total		240	34-78	4-17	18-32		11	29	40	19	18	7	12	4	1	90

TEAM REBS: 17   TOTAL TO: 13

CAVALIERS	POS	MIN	FG-A	3P-A	FT-A	+/-	OFF	DEF	TOT	AST	PF	ST	TO	BS	BA	PTS
L. James	F	39:44	12-18	2-4	1-3	+10	1	5	6	3	3	3	5	0	0	27
K. Love	F	31:43	5-14	3-7	3-6	-1	1	9	10	2	2	0	1	0	2	16
T. Thompson	C	13:23	0-0	0-0	0-0	+4	1	0	1	1	2	0	0	0	0	0
J. Smith	G	34:25	7-13	7-11	0-0	-4	0	5	5	1	4	0	1	0	1	21
K. Irving	G	33:42	8-18	4-7	2-3	-1	1	0	1	4	0	2	1	0	1	22
T. Mozgov		09:07	0-1	0-0	0-0	-2	0	0	0	1	1	0	2	0	0	0
I. Shumpert		17:50	1-4	0-2	0-0	+2	1	5	6	2	2	1	0	0	0	2
R. Jefferson		23:24	1-3	1-3	0-0	+25	1	1	2	3	0	0	0	0	0	3
M. Dellavedova		22:01	3-5	1-1	1-2	+25	0	1	1	9	3	1	1	0	0	8
C. Frye		11:02	1-2	1-2	0-0	+18	0	4	4	0	4	0	1	0	0	3
J. McRae		01:13	2-2	1-1	0-0	+3	0	1	1	0	0	0	0	0	0	5
D. Jones		01:13	0-0	0-0	0-0	+3	0	0	0	0	0	0	0	0	0	0
J. Jones		01:13	0-0	0-0	0-0	+3	0	0	0	0	0	0	0	0	0	0
Total		240	40-80	20-38	7-14		6	31	37	23	24	7	12	1	4	107

TEAM REBS: 11   TOTAL TO: 13

LeBron James celebrates with Kyrie Irving after Irving hit a 3-pointer in Game 3.

GUS CHAN
THE PLAIN DEALER

MUCH TOO GOOD

CHRIS HAYNES | *cleveland.com*
April 22, 2016

The Detroit Pistons knew they had to get this one. No NBA team has ever come back from a 0-3 series deficit. Progress is being made.

This time around on Wednesday evening at The Q, it took them two and a half quarters to put their imprint on the game. A 16-2 run by the reigning Eastern Conference champs in the middle of the third quarter was the difference-maker. It provided enough breathing space that ultimately led to the Cavaliers going up 2-0 with a 107-90 victory in this opening-round playoff series.

LeBron James registered 27 points and six rebounds. Kyrie Irving included 22 points and four assists. J.R. Smith scored 21 points -- all on seven triples.

The Cavaliers hit 20 three-pointers out of 38 attempts, tying an NBA playoff record most recently achieved by the 2015 Warriors. They were on fire.

Before Cleveland made its run, Detroit carried a 10-point lead at one point in the first half. The Pistons are a young, confident, resilient bunch.

The Cavaliers' first lead didn't come until three minutes into the second quarter.

The Big 3 combine for 66 as Cavaliers take 3-0 series lead, 101-91 over Pistons

CAVALIERS	POS	MIN	FG-A	3P-A	FT-A	+/-	OFF	DEF	TOT	AST	PF	ST	TO	BS	BA	PTS
L. James	F	42:55	8-24	1-6	3-5	+17	1	12	13	7	2	0	5	1	1	20
K. Love	F	38:42	7-10	1-3	5-6	+8	2	10	12	2	0	0	1	0	0	20
T. Thompson	C	31:13	4-7	0-0	0-1	+5	8	2	10	1	3	1	1	2	2	8
J. Smith	G	37:01	3-9	3-8	0-0	+15	1	8	9	3	3	1	0	0	0	9
K. Irving	G	39:23	11-20	3-6	1-1	+9	0	0	0	4	1	0	2	0	0	26
I. Shumpert		11:39	2-5	2-3	0-0	0	0	2	2	1	2	1	1	0	0	6
R. Jefferson		14:13	0-0	0-0	0-0	-4	0	0	0	1	2	0	0	0	0	0
C. Frye		08:37	0-0	0-0	0-0	+1	0	0	0	0	1	0	1	0	0	0
M. Dellavedova		16:17	4-5	2-3	2-2	-1	0	0	0	5	3	0	0	0	0	12
D. Jones	DNP - COACH'S DECISION															
J. Jones	DNP - COACH'S DECISION															
T. Mozgov	DNP - COACH'S DECISION															
M. Williams	DNP - COACH'S DECISION															
Total		240	39-80	12-29	11-15		12	34	46	24	17	3	10	4	3	101

TEAM REBS: 5 TOTAL TO: 10

PISTONS	POS	MIN	FG-A	3P-A	FT-A	+/-	OFF	DEF	TOT	AST	PF	ST	TO	BS	BA	PTS
T. Harris	F	42:08	6-10	1-3	0-0	-9	0	7	7	4	5	1	1	1	1	13
M. Morris	F	39:11	5-11	0-2	6-6	-7	0	3	3	3	3	0	1	0	0	16
A. Drummond	C	27:11	8-14	0-0	1-6	0	3	4	7	0	0	0	2	1	17
K. Caldwell-Pope	G	42:42	7-14	3-8	1-1	-10	0	3	3	1	4	1	0	1	18
R. Jackson	G	39:11	5-16	1-8	2-2	-6	0	4	4	12	2	2	1	0	1	13
A. Tolliver		11:10	1-2	0-1	0-0	-1	0	2	2	0	0	0	0	0	0	2
S. Blake		08:49	0-1	0-0	0-0	-4	0	1	1	2	0	0	0	0	0	0
A. Baynes		15:52	1-2	0-0	1-2	-16	2	2	4	1	2	0	3	0	1	3
S. Johnson		13:46	3-4	1-1	2-2	+3	0	1	1	0	3	0	0	0	0	9
J. Anthony	DNP - COACH'S DECISION															
S. Dinwiddie	DNP - COACH'S DECISION															
D. Hilliard	DNP - COACH'S DECISION															
J. Meeks	DNP - COACH'S DECISION															
Total		240	36-74	6-23	13-19		5	27	32	22	19	7	7	3	4	91

TEAM REBS: 6 TOTAL TO: 8

Matthew Dellavedova and LeBron James congratulate Kyrie Irving on a late 3-pointer in Game 4. THOMAS ONDREY | THE PLAIN DEALER

THE PLAIN DEALER

NBA PLAYOFFS | EASTERN CONFERENCE FIRST ROUND | SECTION C | 4 PAGES

SWEEP RELIEF

Irving hits from long range, Cavaliers make short work of the Pistons

BASEBALL TIME IN DETROIT

CHRIS HAYNES | *cleveland.com*

April 24, 2016

Cavaliers sweep into second round, topping Detroit 100-98

It's officially full-time baseball season for fans in the Motor City.

The Cleveland Cavaliers executed the sweep by defeating the Detroit Pistons, 100-98 in Game 4 of the first round at The Palace of Auburn Hills on Sunday to advance to the semifinals.

Kyrie Irving has torched Detroit all series long and it didn't change in the finale. He recorded 31 points on 12-of-24 shooting to go with five assists in 40 minutes. He closed the third quarter with a halfcourt trey and then buried another with 44 seconds left to provide the decisive points.

You knew the Pistons would come out with a sense of desperation. They jumped out to a 10-2 start, as the Cavaliers were a step slow. But a timeout restored the urgency -- along with two quick fouls on Andre Drummond which put the center on the bench -- and they ran off a 15-7 spree that got the game close again. It stayed that way through the rest of the half.

Out of halftime with the Cavaliers up one, Irving decided to take matters into his own hands. He erupted for 10 points in the first five minutes to give his team an 11-point lead, the largest of the night.

PISTONS	POS	MIN	FG-A	3P-A	FT-A	+/-	OFF	DEF	TOT	AST	PF	ST	TO	BS	BA	PTS
L. James	F	41:27	9-19	1-6	3-3	+5	2	9	11	6	4	2	2	0	0	22
K. Love	F	34:36	3-15	1-5	4-4	-2	4	9	13	2	3	1	0	0	0	11
T. Thompson	C	38:22	2-5	0-0	1-2	0	3	2	5	0	3	1	1	1	2	5
J. Smith	G	35:23	5-8	5-7	0-0	+1	0	1	1	0	2	0	0	0	0	15
K. Irving	G	40:25	12-25	4-11	3-4	-2	0	3	3	5	2	1	2	0	0	31
R. Jefferson		16:36	2-6	1-4	0-0	+5	0	4	4	1	2	0	0	0	1	5
I. Shumpert		09:24	0-2	0-1	0-0	+2	1	2	3	1	1	0	0	0	1	0
C. Frye		08:57	0-1	0-0	0-0	+2	0	1	1	0	3	1	0	0	0	0
M. Dellavedova		14:50	3-5	1-2	4-4	-1	0	0	0	1	2	0	0	0	0	11
D. Jones	DNP - COACH'S DECISION															
J. Jones	DNP - COACH'S DECISION															
T. Mozgov	DNP - COACH'S DECISION															
M. Williams	DNP - COACH'S DECISION															
Total		240	36-86	13-36	15-17		10	31	41	16	22	6	5	1	4	100

TEAM REBS: 6 TOTAL TO: 6

CAVALIERS	POS	MIN	FG-A	3P-A	FT-A	+/-	OFF	DEF	TOT	AST	PF	ST	TO	BS	BA	PTS
T. Harris	F	41:17	8-14	2-4	5-5	+6	2	11	13	2	0	0	1	0	0	23
M. Morris	F	31:08	9-12	3-4	3-5	-13	0	1	1	0	5	0	1	0	0	24
A. Drummond	C	31:18	6-13	0-0	5-10	-2	1	10	11	0	2	0	1	2	0	17
K. Caldwell-Pope	G	42:48	3-10	3-5	0-0	+1	2	2	4	5	2	2	0	0	0	9
R. Jackson	G	37:26	6-13	0-6	1-1	+4	0	3	3	12	2	0	5	1	0	13
A. Baynes		10:13	1-3	0-0	0-0	-6	1	2	3	1	2	0	0	0	1	2
S. Johnson		29:35	2-8	1-4	0-0	+7	0	5	5	0	2	1	1	0	0	5
S. Blake		10:34	1-2	1-1	0-0	-6	0	1	1	2	3	0	0	0	0	3
A. Tolliver		05:41	1-1	0-0	0-0	-1	1	0	1	0	0	0	1	0	0	2
J. Anthony	DNP - COACH'S DECISION															
S. Dinwiddie	DNP - COACH'S DECISION															
D. Hilliard	DNP - COACH'S DECISION															
J. Meeks	DNP - COACH'S DECISION															
Total		240	37-76	10-24	14-21		7	35	42	22	18	3	9	4	1	98

TEAM REBS: 9 TOTAL TO: 9

AN OLD FOE FACING THE SAME RESULT

JOE VARDON | *The Plain Dealer*
April 27, 2016

Cavaliers have imposed their will on Hawks for two seasons

The Atlanta Hawks worked really hard for a reward that could look a lot like a punishment next week.

Perhaps no team has felt LeBron James' wrath over the past 12 months more so than the Hawks.

Coming off their four-game sweep of the Detroit Pistons in an Eastern Conference first-round series, James and the Cavs will host Atlanta onMonday in Game 1 of a conference semifinal.

The Hawks dispatched the Boston Celtics in six games in the first round.

Cleveland swept both Atlanta and the Celtics out of the playoffs a year ago. But it was the Hawks upon whose forehead he left his personal footprint.

James averaged 30.3 points, 11.0 rebounds, and 9.3 assists against the Hawks in the East finals last season. No other player in NBA history has ever averaged at least 30 points, 10 rebounds, and nine assists in a playoff series.

In Game 3 of that series, James tallied 37 points, 18 rebounds, and 13 assists. The only other player ever to have a game like that was Wilt Chamberlain, who posted 53 points, 32 rebounds, and 14 assists in a regular-season game in March of 1968.

James crushed the Hawks during the 2015-16 regular season as well, averaging 27.3 points, 11.0 rebounds, and 7.7 assists while shooting 57.9 percent from the field in three games.

The Cavs played a different style with limited personnel against the Hawks in the playoffs. Kevin Love was out for the playoffs and Kyrie Irving hobbled because of injuries (Irving played in just two games), so Cleveland slowed its pace to a crawl and ran everything through James.

Irving and Love are of course back (they averaged 27.3 and 18.8 points against the Pistons last series) and the Cavs play at a much quicker pace.

DeMarre Carroll was on the Hawks' roster last year and is one of the few small forwards in the league who are gifted enough athletically to stay with James. But Carroll injured his knee in Game 1 of the conference finals and struggled to keep up. Carroll's gone (via free agency to Toronto), and the 6-7 Kent Bazemore is an inch shorter and many pounds lighter than James. Those matchups haven't gone well for Bazemore.

Thabo Sefolosha missed the conference finals with a broken leg and is back. He can come off the bench to guard James. Hawks coach Mike Budenholzer could also look to power forward Paul Millsap to guard James (like the Pistons did with power forward Marcus Morris), but that could create a matchup problem for the Hawks with Love.

Tristan Thompson battles two Hawks for a rebound in Game 1.
JOSHUA GUNTER CLEVELAND.COM

Cavaliers 104, Hawks 93 Game 1

CAKEWALK, UNTIL IT'S NOT

CHRIS HAYNES | *cleveland.com*
May 2, 2016

Cavaliers use late run to turn away Hawks rally in series opener

After nearly coughing up an 18-point lead, the Cleveland Cavaliers held on to take Game 1 of the Eastern semifinals with an 104-93 victory over the Atlanta Hawks Monday night at The Q.

It's been a long eight days off for the Cavaliers and rust — or perhaps some fatigue — showed towards the end. A LeBron James steal and eventual dunk gave Cleveland a 72-54 lead midway through the third. But Atlanta's Dennis Schroder, who was shooting 18 percent from three this postseason, hit five of his first seven attempts beyond the arc. That helped the Hawks capture their first lead (80-79) with eight minutes remaining.

A Schroder layup tied the game at 86 — his 27th point of the night — but he asked for some rest with six minutes remaining. Schroder didn't score again, J.R. Smith hit a big 3-pointer and James had a couple of spinning layups and the Cavs were back in control.

Atlanta (0-1) struggled to execute offensively the duration as Cleveland (1-0) cranked up its defensive intensity, forcing three costly turnovers down the stretch. Excluding a meaningless three with 18 seconds left, the Cavaliers prevented the Hawks from scoring a field goal in the last four minutes of the game.

HAWKS			FIELD GOALS				REBOUNDS									
	POS	MIN	FG-A	3P-A	FT-A	+/-	OFF	DEF	TOT	AST	PF	ST	TO	BS	BA	PTS
K. Bazemore	F	35:57	6-14	3-10	1-2	-15	4	8	12	4	4	2	4	0	0	16
P. Millsap	F	39:44	6-19	0-3	5-8	-16	8	5	13	3	3	2	2	4	0	17
A. Horford	C	36:00	4-13	0-1	2-2	-9	0	6	6	1	5	2	1	3	1	10
K. Korver	G	36:45	0-1	0-1	3-3	-6	0	5	5	0	2	0	0	0	3	3
J. Teague	G	21:37	2-9	1-4	3-4	-13	1	1	2	4	1	0	0	0	2	8
T. Sefolosha		11:22	1-3	0-1	0-0	-7	0	1	1	1	1	0	0	0	1	2
M. Scott		15:42	3-3	1-1	0-0	+6	0	4	4	2	1	0	0	0	0	7
D. Schroder		28:33	10-20	5-10	2-2	+3	1	2	3	6	5	0	5	0	2	27
T. Hardaway Jr.		07:37	0-4	0-2	0-0	+2	0	0	0	0	0	0	0	0	0	0
M. Muscala		06:03	0-0	0-0	0-0	-1	1	1	2	0	0	0	0	0	0	0
L. Patterson		00:41	1-1	1-1	0-0	+1	0	0	0	0	0	0	0	0	0	3
K. Hinrich	DNP - COACH'S DECISION															
K. Humphries	DNP - COACH'S DECISION															
Total		240	33-87	11-34	16-21		15	33	48	21	22	6	12	7	7	93

TEAM REBS: 10   TOTAL TO: 12

CAVALIERS			FIELD GOALS				REBOUNDS									
	POS	MIN	FG-A	3P-A	FT-A	+/-	OFF	DEF	TOT	AST	PF	ST	TO	BS	BA	PTS
L. James	F	40:34	11-21	2-4	1-1	+16	0	7	7	9	3	5	4	1	1	25
K. Love	F	37:33	4-17	3-9	6-7	+15	2	9	11	1	2	1	1	1	3	17
T. Thompson	C	40:28	3-6	0-0	2-4	+16	7	7	14	2	1	0	0	2	1	8
J. Smith	G	37:55	4-8	4-7	0-2	+16	1	4	5	3	3	1	0	0	0	12
K. Irving	G	34:24	8-18	3-5	2-2	+17	0	1	1	8	3	1	2	2	2	21
I. Shumpert		14:55	1-2	0-0	0-0	-9	0	1	1	4	0	0	0	0	0	2
M. Dellavedova		13:25	0-2	0-1	1-2	-5	0	1	1	3	0	1	0	0	1	1
C. Frye		09:06	2-5	1-3	3-3	-4	0	0	0	1	0	0	0	0	1	8
R. Jefferson		10:12	3-3	2-2	0-0	-5	0	4	4	0	0	0	0	0	0	8
T. Mozgov		00:07	0-0	0-0	0-0		0	0	0	0	0	0	0	0	0	0
M. Williams		00:41	0-0	0-0	0-0	-1	0	0	0	0	0	0	0	0	0	0
D. Jones		00:41	1-1	0-0	0-0	-1	0	0	0	0	0	1	0	0	0	2
J. Jones	DNP - COACH'S DECISION															
Total		240	37-83	15-31	15-21		10	34	44	27	20	9	8	7	7	104

TEAM REBS: 9   TOTAL TO: 8

J.R. Smith knocks
down one of his seven
3-pointers in Game 2.

JOHN KUNTZ | CLEVELAND.COM

THREE AND EASY

CHRIS HAYNES | *cleveland.com*
May 4, 2016

he Atlanta Hawks are at the midway point from being put out of their misery after suffering an humiliating, record-observing annihilation.

On Wednesday night, the Cleveland Cavaliers set an NBA record with 25 threes splashed in a game (regular season or playoff) that fueled a 123-98 rout of the Hawks in Game 2 of the semifinals round.

The Houston Rockets in 2009 and Orlando Magic in 2013 owned the all-time triple feat at 22 in the regular season. The previous playoff record was still young with the Golden State Warriors holding the mark of 21 only a week and three days.

It was an outside shooting assault. Cleveland (2-0) made it 10 straight victories over Atlanta (0-2). LeBron James registered 27 points, five assists and four threes. Kyrie Irving added 19 points, six assists and four triplets of his own. Kevin Love contributed 11 points, 13 rebounds and three 3-pointers. No other player in the franchise's history has ever recorded a double-double in the first six games of postseason play.

The Cavaliers also connected on a playoff-record 18 treys in the first half. The previous record was 12. The reigning Eastern Conference champs hit 13 in the first 16 minutes of the contest.

Cavaliers set NBA record with 25 3s in routing Hawks, 123-98 to take 2-0 series lead

HAWKS	POS	MIN	FG-A	3P-A	FT-A	+/-	OFF	DEF	TOT	AST	PF	ST	TO	BS	BA	PTS
K. Bazemore	F	26:54	1-7	0-3	3-3	-30	0	1	1	1	1	0	1	0	1	5
P. Millsap	F	26:48	4-8	1-2	7-8	-25	3	8	11	1	3	1	3	1	0	16
A. Horford	C	24:58	3-7	2-3	2-2	-22	0	3	3	2	2	0	2	1	0	10
K. Korver	G	19:30	3-7	1-2	0-0	-27	1	1	0	3	0	0	0	0	7
J. Teague	G	23:02	3-10	0-2	8-9	-17	0	3	3	5	3	0	2	0	0	14
M. Scott		18:53	0-0	0-0	2-2	-16	0	3	3	1	2	0	1	1	0	2
T. Sefolosha		17:52	4-4	2-2	0-0	-14	0	2	2	2	1	0	1	0	0	10
D. Schroder		13:55	2-5	1-3	0-0	-4	1	0	1	3	0	2	0	0	5
T. Hardaway Jr.		17:38	1-5	1-4	1-2	+11	0	2	2	1	0	0	2	0	0	4
M. Muscala		14:23	4-5	2-2	0-0	+4	1	0	1	0	1	0	0	0	0	10
K. Humphries		15:21	4-8	0-1	4-4	+2	3	6	9	1	1	1	0	0	0	12
K. Hinrich		12:00	1-4	1-2	0-0	+11	0	2	2	0	2	0	0	0	0	3
L. Patterson		08:46	0-1	0-1	0-0	+2	0	1	1	1	1	1	2	0	0	0
Total		240	30-71	11-27	27-30		8	32	40	18	23	3	16	3	1	98

TEAM REBS: 6   TOTAL TO: 16

CAVALIERS	POS	MIN	FG-A	3P-A	FT-A	+/-	OFF	DEF	TOT	AST	PF	ST	TO	BS	BA	PTS
L. James	F	28:08	9-15	4-6	5-9	+24	0	4	4	5	4	3	2	0	1	27
K. Love	F	26:29	3-12	3-4	2-2	+25	6	7	13	2	1	0	1	0	2	11
T. Thompson	C	19:19	1-5	0-0	3-4	+18	4	3	7	0	3	0	1	1	0	5
J. Smith		28:28	8-14	7-13	0-0	+29	0	2	2	0	2	2	0	0	23
K. Irving	G	22:40	5-9	4-5	5-6	+17	0	2	2	6	2	1	1	0	0	19
I. Shumpert		18:35	3-3	1-1	0-0	+4	0	2	2	3	2	0	0	0	0	7
R. Jefferson		24:23	3-3	2-2	0-0	+10	0	2	2	3	2	0	2	0	0	8
M. Dellavedova		13:20	1-7	1-3	0-0	+19	1	1	2	6	1	0	0	0	0	3
C. Frye		20:11	5-7	1-3	1-2	+7	1	4	5	2	1	1	0	0	12
T. Mozgov		12:51	0-1	0-0	0-0	-13	0	1	1	0	0	0	0	0	0
M. Williams		12:00	2-5	1-4	0-0	-11	0	1	1	0	2	1	0	0	0	5
J. Jones		07:40	0-4	0-2	0-0	-1	0	1	1	0	0	0	1	0	0	0
D. Jones		05:56	1-2	1-2	0-0	-3	0	1	1	0	0	0	0	0	0	3
Total		240	41-87	25-45	16-23		12	31	43	27	22	8	8	1	3	123

TEAM REBS: 8   TOTAL TO: 10

Channing Frye hit seven
3-pointers and led all scorers in
Game 3 with 27 points.

THOMAS ONDREY | THE PLAIN DEALER

CAVS TOO MUCH IN FOURTH

CHRIS HAYNES | *cleveland.com*
May 6, 2016

Channing Frye, Kyrie Irving and LeBron James dominated a 36-point fourth quarter while the Atlanta Hawks completely unraveled, resulting in a 3-0 series lead after an 121-108 win on Friday.

Atlanta had a six-point lead heading into the fourth quarter built on their best offensive performance of the series. But Irving exploded for 12 of his 24 points in the quarter, Frye hit three of his seven 3-pointers and the team's defensive intensity locked in. The Hawks couldn't get a clean look in a 17-point period, either missing badly or turning the ball over.

The atmosphere went from rowdy to mute in a 12-minute span.

Frye was brought to Cleveland for moments like these. He scored 27 points and was 7-of-9 from downtown. James padded the stat-sheet with 24 points, 13 rebounds and eight assists. Kevin Love has a double-double in every postseason game this year, finishing with 21 points and 15 rebounds — including the team's final 3-pointer that provided a 10-point lead with 96 seconds left.

"We're in a great rhythm right now," Tyronn Lue said. "I think it all starts with trust, sharing the basketball, moving the basketball, not playing a lot of one-on-one isolation basketball."

Cavaliers' 36-point fourth quarter caps Game 3 comeback, 121-108, over Atlanta

CAVALIERS

	POS	MIN	FG-A	3P-A	FT-A	+/-	OFF	DEF	TOT	AST	PF	ST	TO	BS	BA	PTS
L. James	F	38:58	8-16	1-4	7-9	+17	2	11	13	8	2	2	5	0	1	24
K. Love	F	29:14	7-17	5-12	2-2	+9	4	11	15	3	4	0	3	1	0	21
T. Thompson	C	27:46	1-6	0-0	5-12	-14	9	4	13	2	1	0	4	0	1	7
J. Smith	G	35:37	2-4	2-4	0-0	+5	1	2	3	3	2	1	1	0	0	6
K. Irving	G	40:04	9-19	4-5	2-2	+12	0	1	1	3	5	3	2	0	2	24
I. Shumpert		17:10	2-3	1-1	0-2	+6	1	1	2	4	0	1	0	0	1	5
M. Dellavedova		12:25	1-4	1-3	0-0	+5	0	1	1	2	3	0	1	0	1	3
C. Frye		28:08	10-13	7-9	0-0	+28	1	6	7	0	3	1	2	0	1	27
R. Jefferson		09:38	2-3	0-1	0-0	-3	0	0	0	1	1	1	0	0	0	4
D. Jones		00:30	0-0	0-0	0-0		0	0	0	0	0	0	0	0	0	0
M. Williams		00:30	0-0	0-0	0-0		0	0	0	0	0	0	0	0	0	0
J. Jones	DNP - COACH'S DECISION															
T. Mozgov	DNP - COACH'S DECISION															
Total		240	42-85	21-39	16-27		18	37	55	26	21	9	18	1	7	121

TEAM REBS: 10   TOTAL TO: 20

HAWKS

	POS	MIN	FG-A	3P-A	FT-A	+/-	OFF	DEF	TOT	AST	PF	ST	TO	BS	BA	PTS
T. Sefolosha	F	29:17	3-5	2-2	0-0	-1	1	3	4	2	2	1	0	0	0	8
P. Millsap	F	39:10	7-17	1-4	2-3	-8	3	5	8	4	2	2	4	1	0	17
A. Horford	C	31:26	11-15	2-4	0-0	-26	0	1	1	3	3	2	3	0	0	24
K. Bazemore	G	30:58	1-5	1-3	0-0	-23	1	3	4	1	3	2	2	0	0	3
J. Teague	G	36:09	7-17	2-6	3-4	-11	0	1	1	14	3	0	1	0	1	19
K. Humphries		19:42	4-9	1-3	0-0	+12	1	3	4	1	3	1	1	2	0	9
K. Korver		32:22	6-11	5-9	1-1	-2	0	3	3	0	1	0	1	1	0	18
D. Schroder		11:51	2-5	2-3	2-2	-2	0	2	2	4	2	0	2	0	0	8
T. Hardaway Jr.		02:53	0-0	0-0	2-2		0	0	0	0	0	0	0	0	0	2
M. Muscala		01:05	0-0	0-0	0-0		0	0	0	0	0	0	0	0	0	0
M. Scott		05:07	0-0	0-0	0-0	-4	0	1	1	0	2	0	0	0	0	0
K. Hinrich	DNP - COACH'S DECISION															
L. Patterson	DNP - COACH'S DECISION															
Total		240	41-84	16-34	10-12		6	22	28	29	21	8	14	7	1	108

TEAM REBS: 6   TOTAL TO: 14

LeBron James is mobbed by teammates after Game 4

SWEEP DREAMS

CHRIS HAYNES | *cleveland.com*
May 8, 2016

Cavaliers forward LeBron James easily wins a jump ball in the final seconds against Hawks guard Dennis Schroder on Sunday. THOMAS ONDREY / THE PLAIN DEALER

Whenever the Cleveland Cavaliers have gone up 3-0 in a series, they've never failed to sweep the opposition.

The wine and gold have advanced to the Eastern Conference Finals for the second consecutive year after eliminating the Atlanta Hawks with a tough 100-99 victory Sunday at Philips Arena.

Kevin Love showed no love for the Hawks. He went off for 27 points and 13 rebounds while hitting eight 3-pointers. He has supplied a double-double in every game this postseason.

LeBron James just missed a triple-double with 21 points, 10 rebounds and nine assists.

Kyrie Irving contributed 21 points and eight assists.

This game was a wild one.

The Hawks' Paul Millsap came out with a vengeance. He scored 15 of his 19 points in the first quarter to give his team a nine-point advantage. Atlanta extended its lead to 12 in the second quarter in a desperate effort to prolong this series.

Cavaliers coach Tyronn Lue foresaw that the Hawks would come strong from the onset.

"We know they're going to play hard at the start," he said before the game. "So we've just got to try to weather the storm."

Cleveland improves to 8-0 in the postseason and completes another sweep of Atlanta

CAVALIERS	POS	MIN	FIELD GOALS				REBOUNDS									
			FG-A	3P-A	FT-A	+/-	OFF	DEF	TOT	AST	PF	ST	TO	BS	BA	PTS
L. James	F	37:52	10-23	1-5	0-3	+2	5	5	10	9	2	2	6	1	4	21
K. Love	F	37:16	9-25	8-15	1-1	+14	3	10	13	4	1	0	2	0	1	27
T. Thompson	C	29:23	2-3	0-0	1-2	+9	4	6	10	0	3	1	1	2	0	5
J. Smith	G	35:31	1-4	1-4	0-0	+1	0	2	2	0	2	1	2	2	0	3
K. Irving	G	42:20	8-16	1-3	4-5	+7	0	2	2	8	0	0	2	1	1	21
C. Frye		19:38	3-6	2-4	0-0	-17	0	1	1	1	2	0	1	1	0	8
R. Jefferson		04:03	1-3	1-1	0-0	-9	0	0	0	0	1	0	0	0	1	3
M. Dellavedova		15:28	1-2	0-1	0-0	-6	0	0	0	1	0	0	0	0	0	2
I. Shumpert		18:29	3-6	2-4	2-2	+4	2	1	3	0	3	2	1	0	0	10
D. Jones		DNP - COACH'S DECISION														
J. Jones		DNP - COACH'S DECISION														
T. Mozgov		DNP - COACH'S DECISION														
M. Williams		DNP - COACH'S DECISION														
Total		240	38-88	16-37	8-13		14	27	41	23	14	6	15	7	7	100

TEAM REBS: 10   TOTAL TO: 15

HAWKS	POS	MIN	FIELD GOALS				REBOUNDS									
			FG-A	3P-A	FT-A	+/-	OFF	DEF	TOT	AST	PF	ST	TO	BS	BA	PTS
T. Sefolosha	F	32:28	7-12	2-3	0-2	-7	3	3	6	3	3	2	2	1	0	16
P. Millsap	F	41:29	5-12	1-4	8-10	+3	2	7	9	3	3	1	3	1	1	19
A. Horford	C	39:10	7-14	1-5	0-0	-7	0	4	4	4	2	0	2	1	0	15
K. Bazemore	G	38:56	5-12	1-7	0-0	-11	0	7	7	2	0	3	0	0	1	11
J. Teague	G	22:00	2-5	1-3	0-0	-10	0	2	2	2	1	3	0	0	5
K. Humphries		12:16	2-5	2-4	2-2	+3	2	5	7	1	2	0	0	3	0	8
K. Korver		24:36	1-4	0-2	0-0	+16	1	3	4	1	2	1	0	2	2	2
D. Schroder		25:46	10-18	1-3	0-0	+11	1	2	3	6	2	2	1	0	2	21
M. Scott		03:19	1-1	0-0	0-0	-3	0	0	0	0	0	0	0	0	0	2
T. Hardaway Jr.		DNP - COACH'S DECISION														
K. Hinrich		DNP - COACH'S DECISION														
M. Muscala		DNP - COACH'S DECISION														
L. Patterson		DNP - COACH'S DECISION														
Total		240	40-83	9-31	10-14		9	33	42	22	16	10	12	7	7	99

TEAM REBS: 9   TOTAL TO: 13

UNLOCKED POTENTIAL

Every 3-point shot the Cavaliers hit in their four-game sweep of the Hawks.

GAME 1 **CAVS 104, HAWKS 93** (AT CLEVELAND)

J.R. Smith
Assist: James
11:12, 1Q
CLE 5, ATL 2

LeBron James
Assist: Love
9:05, 1Q
CLE 10, ATL 5

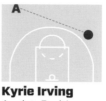

Kyrie Irving
Assist: None
8:05, 1Q
CLE 13, ATL 8

Kyrie Irving
Assist: Smith
7:41, 1Q
CLE 16, ATL 8

J.R. Smith
Assist: Thompson
1:05, 1Q
CLE 27, ATL 19

Channing Frye
Assist: Dellavedova
0:02, 1Q
CLE 30, ATL 19

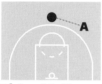

Richard Jefferson
Assist: James
9:38, 2Q
CLE 35, ATL 22

Kevin Love
Assist: Irving
7:22, 2Q
CLE 38, ATL 27

Richard Jefferson
Assist: James
6:20, 2Q
CLE 41, ATL 29

J.R. Smith
Assist: Irving
11:31, 3Q
CLE 54, ATL 41

LeBron James
Assist: Irving
6:14, 3Q
CLE 63, ATL 51

Kevin Love
Assist: James
5:34, 3Q
CLE 66, ATL 52

Kevin Love
Assist: James
4:24, 3Q
CLE 70, ATL 52

Kyrie Irving
Assist: James
7:37, 4Q
CLE 82, ATL 80

J.R. Smith
Assist: James
4:06, 4Q
CLE 90, ATL 88

JOSH CRUTCHMER
THE PLAIN DEALER

SOURCE: NBA.com

● Made shot
A Assist
X Missed shot

GAME 2 **CAVS 123, HAWKS 98** (AT CLEVELAND)

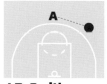

J.R. Smith
Assist: Irving
8:59, 1Q
CLE 5, ATL 7

Kevin Love
Assist: Irving
6:54 1Q
CLE 13, ATL 11

Kyrie Irving
Assist: James
6:30, 1Q
CLE 16, ATL 11

LeBron James
Assist: Irving
4:10, 1Q
CLE 21, ATL 16

Kevin Love
Assist: Irving
3:40, 1Q
CLE 24, ATL 16

J.R. Smith
Assist: James
3:06, 1Q
CLE 27, ATL 16

J.R. Smith
Assist: Jefferson
2:28, 1Q
CLE 30, ATL 16

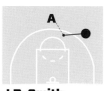

J.R. Smith
Assist: Dellavedova
0:03, 1Q
CLE 35, ATL 20

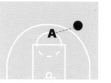

LeBron James
Assist: Dellavedova
11:13, 2Q
CLE 38, ATL 20

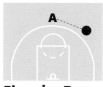

Channing Frye
Assist: James
10:16, 2Q
CLE 41, ATL 23

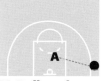

M. Dellavedova
Assist: James
8:47, 2Q
CLE 46, ATL 25

Richard Jefferson
Assist: Shumpert
8:09, 2Q
CLE 49, ATL 25

LeBron James
Assist: None
7:37, 2Q
CLE 52, ATL 27

Kyrie Irving
Assist: Frye
4:35, 2Q
CLE 59, ATL 35

J.R. Smith
Assist: None
3:59, 2Q
CLE 62, ATL 36

J.R. Smith
Assist: Love
2:33, 2Q
CLE 66, ATL 36

Richard Jefferson
Assist: Dellavedova
1:44, 2Q
CLE 71, ATL 36

Kevin Love
Assist: Dellavedova
0:15, 2Q
CLE 74, ATL 36

J.R. Smith
Assist: Irving
9:43, 3Q
CLE 81, ATL 43

LeBron James
Assist: Irving
9:25, 3Q
CLE 84, ATL 43

Kyrie Irving
Assist: James
5:37, 3Q
CLE 93, ATL 58

Kyrie Irving
Assist: None
5:06, 3Q
CLE 96, ATL 60

Iman Shumpert
Assist: None
7:20, 4Q
CLE 115, ATL 86

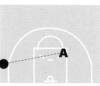

James Jones
Assist: Jefferson
2:22, 4Q
CLE 120, ATL 96

Mo Williams
Assist: None
1:50, 4Q
CLE 123, ATL 96

UNLOCKED POTENTIAL

Every 3-point shot the Cavaliers hit in their four-game sweep of the Hawks.

GAME 3 **CAVS 121, HAWKS 108** (AT ATLANTA)

Kevin Love
Assist: James
11:24, 1Q
CLE 3, ATL 2

Kevin Love
Assist: Irving
9:33, 1Q
CLE 6, ATL 8

Kevin Love
Assist: Smith
7:24, 1Q
CLE 13, ATL 13

J.R. Smith
Assist: Love
6:13, 1Q
CLE 18, ATL 13

M. Dellavedova
Assist: Shumpert
1:14, 1Q
CLE 26, ATL 24

Channing Frye
Assist: Shumpert
0:51, 1Q
CLE 29, ATL 24

Channing Frye
Assist: Jefferson
11:32, 2Q
CLE 34, ATL 28

Channing Frye
Assist: James
9:04, 2Q
CLE 41, ATL 33

Iman Shumpert
Assist: James
6:32, 2Q
CLE 46, ATL 40

Kevin Love
Assist: Thompson
10:00, 3Q
CLE 61, ATL 68

Channing Frye
Assist: James
8:26, 3Q
CLE 65, ATL 72

Kyrie Irving
Assist: Thompson
7:44, 3Q
CLE 68, ATL 74

J.R. Smith
Assist: James
6:05, 3Q
CLE 73, ATL 77

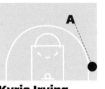

Kyrie Irving
Assist: Smith
4:03, 3Q
CLE 77, ATL 83

Channing Frye
Assist: Dellavedova
10:59, 4Q
CLE 88, ATL 94

Kyrie Irving
Assist: None
10:08, 4Q
CLE 93, ATL 96

Kyrie Irving
Assist: None
9:02, 4Q
CLE 96, ATL 101

Channing Frye
Assist: Irving
8:39, 4Q
CLE 99, ATL 101

Kyrie Irving
Assist: None
9:02, 4Q
CLE 96, ATL 101

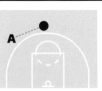

Channing Frye
Assist: Irving
8:39, 4Q
CLE 99, ATL 101

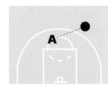

LeBron James
Assist: Smith
6:23, 4Q
CLE 104, ATL 103

Channing Frye
Assist: Love
3:35, 4Q
CLE 113, ATL 104

Kevin Love
Assist: James
1:36, 4Q
CLE 116, ATL 106

JOSH CRUTCHMER
THE PLAIN DEALER

SOURCE: NBA.com

● Made shot
A Assist
X Missed shot

Eastern Conference semifinals Cavaliers 4, Hawks 0

GAME 4 **CAVS 100, HAWKS 99** (AT ATLANTA)

Kevin Love
Assist: James
11:06, 1Q
CLE 3, ATL 3

Kyrie Irving
Assist: None
10:31, 1Q
CLE 6, ATL 5

J.R. Smith
Assist: James
9:33, 1Q
CLE 11, ATL 7

Channing Frye
Assist: James
4:16, 1Q
CLE 22, ATL 20

Richard Jefferson
Assist: Frye
3:03, 1Q
CLE 25, ATL 25

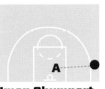

Iman Shumpert
Assist: Love
10:11, 2Q
CLE 31, ATL 40

Kevin Love
Assist: Irving
9:10, 2Q
CLE 34, ATL 42

Kevin Love
Assist: Irving
8:42, 2Q
CLE 37, ATL 44

Kevin Love
Assist: Irving
7:09, 2Q
CLE 44, ATL 48

Iman Shumpert
Assist: Irving
3:28, 2Q
CLE 50, ATL 52

LeBron James
Assist: Irving
10:13, 3Q
CLE 59, ATL 62

Kevin Love
Assist: James
9:47, 3Q
CLE 62, ATL 62

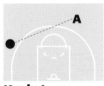

Kevin Love
Assist: James
9:11, 3Q
CLE 65, ATL 64

Kevin Love
Assist: James
8:46, 3Q
CLE 68, ATL 66

Kevin Love
Assist: None
2:16, 3Q
CLE 78, ATL 75

Channing Frye
Assist: James
3:07, 4Q
CLE 96, ATL 91

SERIES 77-152 ON 3-POINTERS

Makes (77)
Per game: 19.25
Most makes:
Kevin Love (19)

Misses (75)
Per game: 18.75
Most misses:
Kevin Love (21)

JOSH CRUTCHMER
THE PLAIN DEALER

SOURCE: NBA.com

● Made shot
A Assist
X Missed shot

LEBRON: CAVS 'UNDERSTAND WHAT WE WANT'

JOE VARDON | *cleveland.com*
May 12, 2016

L eBron James says we're making too much of the Cavaliers' obvious, positive team chemistry.

Does he include in that group of those making too big a deal about it general manager David Griffin, who remarked to cleveland.com's Chris Haynes over the weekend that the players' genuine affection for each other "wasn't there before"?

"We've always been close no matter if it was the postseason or the regular season," James said Wednesday after practice. Cleveland is waiting to play either the Heat or Raptors in the Eastern finals.

"We've always been a close group since we came together last year," James said. "But I think as you continue to have games, continue to have road trips, things of that nature, it's human nature to get close when you're around someone every single day. So, we've always been a close group."

There's little value in arguing the point with James.

What is inarguably true is the Cavs are close now. They've won eight straight to begin the postseason, and are playing better as a team than probably at any point since James returned to Cleveland, including last year's run to the Finals.

The players go crazy for each other on the bench when one makes a play. They go to lunch together on off days and hang at James' house during down time between series.

Reporters traveling with the Cavs saw James and several teammates leave the Four Seasons hotel in Atlanta for lunch on Saturday between games 3 and 4. Usually, media does not frequent the team hotel – reporters were invited there to interview James and coach Tyronn Lue on the off day – so we don't really know if lunching and hanging is something the Cavs have always done together.

And to James' point, there is evidence that at times throughout the past two seasons the players did genuinely seem to enjoy each other's company. Who can forget, for instance, the pics from James' Halloween Party?

But to the many pairs of eyes paid to watch the Cavs each and every day – both inside and outside the organization – something is obviously there that wasn't before. There's a certain trust between James, Kyrie Irving and Kevin Love. It extends upward to Lue and filters downward to Cleveland's capable role players.

Before arguing that this iteration of the Cavs has always been close, James actually gave away that something has indeed changed among the players, for the better.

He said: "We understand what we want, and guys are just taking that seriously and putting in the work."

Halfway to the goal, and the Cavaliers are putting teammates above all else

LeBron James throws down a dunk
in the first half of Game 1.
JOSHUA GUNTER | CLEVELAND.COM

Cavaliers 115, Raptors 84 Game 1

FROM OUTSIDE TO INSIDE

CHRIS HAYNES | *cleveland.com*
May 17, 2016

T he Cleveland Cavaliers have proved during this postseason that they can really shoot the ball from the outside. Now they've proved they can really score from inside.

On Tuesday evening in Game 1 of the Eastern Conference Finals, the Cavaliers embarrassed the Toronto Raptors and their scheme by way of a 115-84 throttling. Cleveland (1-0) took what the defense gave them and attacked the rim in scoring a whopping 56 points in the paint. Toronto (0-1) didn't want to be on the receiving end of a three-point whipping, so they chose to give up dunks and layups.

Kyrie Irving played so aggressively, but yet under control. He registered 18 of his game-high 27 points on 11-of-17 from the floor to go with five assists. LeBron James put in 24 points, six rebounds and four assists. All of his 11 field goals were from right under the basket. He feasted.

Cleveland outrebounded Toronto, 45-23, and shot 55 percent from the field. Cleveland was only 7-of-20 from three-point range, but it didn't matter. The Cavaliers have other methods of winning games.

The Raptors officially have a problem.

Cavaliers dominate paint, throttle Raptors in Game 1, 115-84

RAPTORS	POS	MIN	FG-A	3P-A	FT-A	+/-	OFF	DEF	TOT	AST	PF	ST	TO	BS	BA	PTS
D. Carroll	F	19:38	1-5	0-3	0-0	-15	1	0	1	1	5	2	1	1	0	2
P. Patterson	F	27:47	3-8	1-4	1-2	-16	0	2	2	4	2	0	1	0	0	8
B. Biyombo	C	30:49	5-5	0-0	2-2	-22	2	2	4	0	2	2	2	0	0	12
D. DeRozan	G	34:36	9-17	0-1	0-0	-22	0	0	0	5	1	0	3	0	1	18
K. Lowry	G	31:35	4-14	0-7	0-0	-16	0	4	4	5	2	0	4	0	0	8
J. Johnson		19:38	4-6	2-2	0-0	-6	1	3	4	1	4	1	2	0	0	10
T. Ross		18:54	1-5	1-3	1-2	-23	0	1	1	0	2	1	1	0	0	4
C. Joseph		15:06	1-6	0-2	2-4	-20	0	1	1	3	3	1	0	0	2	4
L. Scola		14:19	1-2	1-1	4-4	-7	0	2	2	0	4	0	0	0	1	7
D. Wright		09:42	1-2	0-0	5-6	-4	0	1	1	0	1	0	1	0	0	7
J. Thompson		05:53	0-1	0-0	0-0	-2	0	0	0	0	0	0	0	0	0	0
N. Powell		06:24	2-4	0-1	0-0	-2	0	2	2	0	0	0	0	0	0	4
L. Nogueira		05:39	0-1	0-0	0-0	0	0	1	1	0	0	0	0	0	0	0
Total		240	32-76	5-24	15-20		4	19	23	19	25	8	14	1	4	84

TEAM REBS: 12   TOTAL TO: 14

CAVALIERS	POS	MIN	FG-A	3P-A	FT-A	+/-	OFF	DEF	TOT	AST	PF	ST	TO	BS	BA	PTS
L. James	F	28:18	11-13	0-1	2-4	+20	2	4	6	4	3	2	4	1	0	24
K. Love	F	27:33	4-8	2-4	4-4	+12	0	4	4	3	1	2	0	0	0	14
T. Thompson	C	28:09	1-4	0-0	4-4	+8	5	2	7	0	2	1	2	0	0	6
J. Smith	G	27:23	1-5	0-3	3-4	+11	0	2	2	3	0	2	0	0	0	5
K. Irving	G	30:07	11-17	1-3	4-4	+15	0	2	2	5	2	2	2	2	0	27
I. Shumpert		21:45	3-4	1-1	1-2	+24	0	3	3	2	1	1	1	0	0	8
R. Jefferson		21:30	2-6	0-2	5-6	+20	2	9	11	1	2	0	1	0	0	9
M. Dellavedova		14:15	3-4	1-1	2-3	+18	0	1	1	3	2	0	3	0	1	9
C. Frye		12:51	3-5	2-3	0-0	+17	0	3	3	1	0	0	0	0	0	8
M. Williams		08:57	1-3	0-0	1-2	+4	0	2	2	0	0	1	0	0	0	3
J. Jones		06:24	0-1	0-1	0-0	+2	0	0	0	0	1	0	0	0	0	0
T. Mozgov		06:24	1-3	0-0	0-0	+2	1	3	4	0	4	0	1	0	0	2
D. Jones		06:24	0-1	0-1	0-0	+2	0	0	0	0	1	0	0	0	0	0
Total		240	41-74	7-20	26-33		10	35	45	22	20	9	16	4	1	115

TEAM REBS: 9   TOTAL TO: 17

LeBron James slams home a
reverse dunk on a fast break.
JOHN KUNTZ | CLEVELAND.COM

PERFECT TEN

CHRIS HAYNES | *cleveland.com*
May 19, 2016

The Cleveland Cavaliers continue to assault the Eastern Conference opposition and Thursday night was no different.

Cleveland took a 2-0 lead in the Eastern Conference Finals with a 108-89 victory over the Toronto Raptors. That's a 10-0 postseason record for the defending conference champs.

The Big 3 combined for 68 points. LeBron James captured his 15th career postseason triple-double by producing 23 points, 11 rebounds and 10 assists in 33 minutes. All 17 of his field goals in these two games have come inside the paint. Kyrie Irving scored 26 points and Kevin Love supplied 19 points and five boards.

The Cavaliers outscored the Raptors in every quarter for the second game in a row.

Coming in, the Raptors had not lost consecutive games during the postseason. To try a new wrinkle, Luis Scola got the start at power forward in place of Patrick Patterson. Raptors head coach Dwane Casey said his team was in a good place before the game.

"Well, other than getting spanked by 30 [on Tuesday], you know, we've been there before," Casey said. "We lost the first game in the other two series. They understand the moment."

Cavaliers' Big 3 leads the way for a 2-0 series lead over Toronto, improving to 10-0 in postseason

RAPTORS	POS	MIN	FG-A	3P-A	FT-A	+/-	OFF	DEF	TOT	AST	PF	ST	TO	BS	BA	PTS
D. Carroll	F	21:36	2-6	1-3	2-2	-9	0	5	5	1	3	0	0	1	1	7
L. Scola	F	14:11	1-5	1-4	3-4	-13	1	2	3	1	2	0	0	0	0	6
B. Biyombo	C	28:54	1-3	0-0	1-1	-4	2	3	5	0	4	0	2	0	3	3
D. DeRozan	G	36:00	8-18	0-0	6-6	-11	0	5	5	2	4	1	2	0	0	22
K. Lowry	G	33:12	4-14	1-8	1-2	-7	1	5	6	3	4	1	5	0	1	10
P. Patterson		28:37	2-5	2-4	0-0	-15	0	1	1	4	4	0	1	1	0	6
T. Ross		16:30	4-10	2-6	1-2	-5	1	1	2	1	4	2	1	0	0	11
C. Joseph		26:54	5-10	1-4	0-0	-17	1	4	5	3	1	2	1	0	0	11
J. Johnson		19:20	5-7	1-2	0-1	-7	0	3	3	1	2	0	0	0	0	11
J. Thompson		04:01	0-0	0-0	0-0	-2	0	0	0	0	2	0	1	0	0	0
D. Wright		05:01	0-1	0-1	0-0	-3	1	1	1	1	0	1	0	0	0	0
N. Powell		03:19	1-3	0-1	0-0	0	0	1	1	0	0	0	0	0	0	2
L. Nogueira		02:25	0-0	0-0	0-0	-2	1	0	1	0	0	0	0	0	0	0
Total		240	33-82	9-33	14-18		7	31	38	17	31	6	12	4	2	89

TEAM REBS: 6   TOTAL TO: 12

CAVALIERS	POS	MIN	FG-A	3P-A	FT-A	+/-	OFF	DEF	TOT	AST	PF	ST	TO	BS	BA	PTS
L. James	F	33:45	7-13	0-2	9-17	+16	1	10	11	11	2	3	2	0	0	23
K. Love	F	30:37	5-8	1-2	8-9	+14	0	5	5	3	1	0	2	1	0	19
T. Thompson	C	30:21	2-5	0-0	5-6	+16	2	10	12	0	2	0	0	1	1	9
J. Smith	G	27:00	4-7	3-5	1-2	+20	1	2	3	0	2	0	0	0	0	12
K. Irving	G	36:57	12-22	0-3	2-3	+13	1	3	4	3	2	1	3	0	1	26
I. Shumpert		23:33	1-2	1-2	0-0	-4	0	1	1	1	2	1	1	0	0	3
R. Jefferson		21:14	1-4	0-0	0-0	+2	1	3	4	1	1	0	0	0	1	2
C. Frye		15:19	4-7	2-4	0-0	+12	1	3	4	0	2	0	0	0	0	10
M. Dellavedova		07:58	0-3	0-1	0-0	+6	0	0	3	1	0	1	0	1	0	0
J. Jones		03:19	0-1	0-1	0-0	0	0	0	0	0	0	0	0	0	0	0
T. Mozgov		03:19	1-1	0-0	0-0	0	0	1	1	0	1	0	0	0	0	2
D. Jones		03:19	1-1	0-0	0-0	0	0	1	1	0	0	0	0	0	0	2
M. Williams		03:19	0-2	0-1	0-0	0	0	0	0	0	0	0	0	0	0	0
Total		240	38-76	7-21	25-37		7	39	46	24	16	5	9	2	4	108

TEAM REBS: 13   TOTAL TO: 11

Toronto's Bismack Biyombo
contests a LeBron James shot
in Game 3.

THOMAS ONDREY | THE PLAIN DEALER

'WE THE NORTH' STRIKES BACK

CHRIS HAYNES | *cleveland.com*
May 21, 2016

Bismack Biyombo just wanted it more, and his determination and will to win helped his team stay in the series Saturday night against the defending Eastern Conference champions.

The Toronto Raptors took Game 3 of the Eastern finals by defeating the Cleveland Cavaliers, 99-84, Saturday night at Air Canada Centre. Cleveland now leads the series 2-1 and lost its first game of the postseason after winning 10 straight.

Biyombo supplied seven points and a franchise-record 26 rebounds to go with four blocks. He was the difference maker. Raptors head coach Dwane Casey said he stressed to his team before the game that beating the Cavaliers is possible.

"The thing I keep reminding everyone, we're in the final four, conference finals," he said. "We won 56 games. We beat this team two out of three times during the regular season."

The Cavs shot just 28-for-79 from the field, 35.4 percent, their worst percentage of the playoffs. Cavs guard Kyrie Irving was 3-for-19, including 1-for-7 on 3-pointers.

The Cavs' Kevin Love had the worst postseason game of his career, going 1-for-9 from the field. He did not play in the fourth quarter.

Raptors, led by Bismack Biyombo, take 99-84 Game 3 victory

Toronto center Bismack Biyombo blocks a shot by Kyrie Irving in the first half Saturday night. Biyombo finished with four blocks and 26 rebounds.

NORTHERN BLIGHT

Cavaliers go cold as Raptors bring emphatic end to perfect playoff run

CAVALIERS	POS	MIN	FG-A	3P-A	FT-A	+/-	OFF	DEF	TOT	AST	PF	ST	TO	BS	BA	PTS
L. James	F	38:50	9-17	1-5	5-7	-11	4	4	8	5	3	2	2	0	1	24
K. Love	F	29:17	1-9	1-4	0-0	-6	0	4	4	2	0	0	0	1	0	3
T. Thompson	C	25:29	0-1	0-0	0-0	0	2	6	8	2	2	0	1	2	1	0
J. Smith	G	37:27	7-16	6-15	2-2	-10	0	5	5	0	1	1	0	0	0	22
K. Irving	G	37:41	3-19	1-7	6-6	-14	1	3	4	1	2	1	3	0	2	13
I. Shumpert		22:21	1-2	1-1	0-0	-8	0	4	4	2	1	0	1	1	0	3
C. Frye		20:53	4-5	3-4	0-0	-13	0	3	3	0	1	3	0	1	0	11
R. Jefferson		08:55	2-4	0-2	1-1	-3	0	2	2	0	0	0	1	0	0	5
M. Dellavedova		12:35	0-4	0-1	0-0	-1	1	1	2	3	0	0	1	0	0	0
D. Jones		01:38	0-0	0-0	0-0	-1	0	0	0	0	0	0	0	0	0	0
M. Williams		01:38	1-2	1-2	0-0	-1	0	0	0	0	0	0	0	0	0	3
J. Jones		01:38	0-0	0-0	0-0	-1	0	0	0	0	0	0	0	0	0	0
T. Mozgov		01:38	0-0	0-0	0-0	-1	0	0	0	0	0	0	0	0	0	0
Total		240	28-79	14-41	14-16		8	32	40	15	10	7	9	5	4	84

TEAM REBS: 3   TOTAL TO: 9

RAPTORS	POS	MIN	FG-A	3P-A	FT-A	+/-	OFF	DEF	TOT	AST	PF	ST	TO	BS	BA	PTS
D. Carroll	F	27:32	4-11	2-7	0-0	+7	1	3	4	1	1	0	2	0	0	10
L. Scola		16:34	0-2	0-1	0-0	0	0	0	0	1	2	0	1	0	0	0
B. Biyombo	C	39:05	3-6	0-0	1-2	+12	8	18	26	1	3	0	1	4	2	7
D. DeRozan	G	40:13	12-24	0-1	8-9	+9	0	5	5	4	1	0	0	0	1	32
K. Lowry	G	32:36	7-13	4-8	2-2	+8	1	5	6	3	4	0	3	0	1	20
C. Joseph		31:17	6-10	2-3	0-0	+14	1	4	5	3	3	0	2	0	0	14
T. Ross		12:22	1-5	1-3	0-0	+4	0	1	1	0	1	0	0	0	1	3
P. Patterson		29:40	4-10	2-6	0-0	+16	1	5	6	1	2	1	0	0	0	10
J. Johnson		10:41	1-2	1-2	0-0	0	0	1	1	0	0	0	0	0	0	3
L. Nogueira		DNP - COACH'S DECISION														
N. Powell		DNP - COACH'S DECISION														
J. Thompson		DNP - COACH'S DECISION														
D. Wright		DNP - COACH'S DECISION														
Total		240	38-83	12-31	11-13		12	42	54	15	17	1	9	4	5	99

TEAM REBS: 3   TOTAL TO: 10

Toronto's Kyle Lowry lit up the Cavs for 35 points in Game 4.

Raptors 105, Cavaliers 99 Game 4

FIT TO BE TIED

CHRIS HAYNES | *cleveland.com*
May 23, 2016

The Cleveland Cavaliers have now officially faced some adversity in these playoffs.

The Toronto Raptors tied the series at two games apiece by winning 105-99 in Game 4 of the Eastern Conference Finals on Monday at Air Canada Centre. Cleveland almost overcame an 18-point deficit, but couldn't hold on down the stretch.

The Toronto backcourt of Kyle Lowry and DeMar DeRozan went for 35 points and 32 points, respectively. The Cavs' LeBron James said he had a secret approach he was looking to execute. He started off guarding DeRozan, instead of J.R. Smith guarding him. DeRozan came into the game averaging 24.0 points in this series. Defense must not have been James' secret.

The Cavaliers struggled mightily from long distance, shooting 13-for-41 from beyond the arc, 31.7 percent. It was by far their worst shooting display of the postseason. It's one thing to be off offensively, but Cleveland compounded the problem by playing abysmal defense in the second quarter.

Lowry got wide-open looks after wide-open looks in the quarter. The Cavaliers' defensive rotations were non-existent.

Lowry, DeRozan earn Raptors another win, take series back to Cleveland square at 2

CAVALIERS	POS	MIN	FG-A	3P-A	FT-A	+/-	OFF	DEF	TOT	AST	PF	ST	TO	BS	BA	PTS
L. James	F	45:48	11-16	1-3	6-6	-4	4	5	9	6	3	2	1	1	0	29
K. Love	F	30:39	4-14	2-7	0-0	-5	1	6	7	3	0	0	1	0	1	10
T. Thompson	C	29:02	1-3	0-0	0-0	-14	3	6	9	0	3	1	2	0	1	2
J. Smith	G	32:02	3-12	3-11	0-0	-5	0	2	2	1	2	0	1	0	1	9
K. Irving	G	38:41	11-21	3-8	1-1	-9	0	3	3	6	3	1	4	0	0	26
C. Frye		21:22	4-8	4-8	0-0	+5	1	5	6	1	3	0	0	0	0	12
I. Shumpert		12:09	0-1	0-1	1-2	0	1	0	1	0	1	1	0	0	0	1
M. Dellavedova		15:29	1-4	0-3	0-0	-3	0	1	1	5	2	0	1	1	0	2
R. Jefferson		14:49	4-4	0-0	0-0	0	0	0	0	1	0	0	0	0	0	8
D. Jones	DND - SUSPENDED															
J. Jones	DNP - COACH'S DECISION															
T. Mozgov	DNP - COACH'S DECISION															
M. Williams	DNP - COACH'S DECISION															
Total		240	39-83	13-41	8-9		10	28	38	23	17	5	10	2	3	99

TEAM REBS: 7   TOTAL TO: 11

RAPTORS	POS	MIN	FG-A	3P-A	FT-A	+/-	OFF	DEF	TOT	AST	PF	ST	TO	BS	BA	PTS
D. Carroll	F	36:16	3-12	1-7	4-5	+11	2	1	3	2	1	0	0	0	0	11
L. Scola	F	14:14	0-1	0-1	0-0	-1	0	0	0	0	2	1	0	0	0	0
B. Biyombo	C	41:42	2-4	0-0	1-4	+8	3	11	14	1	3	0	1	3	0	5
D. DeRozan	G	39:55	14-23	0-1	4-4	+11	0	3	3	3	2	1	2	0	1	32
K. Lowry	G	44:15	14-20	4-7	3-4	+5	1	4	5	5	4	3	2	0	0	35
P. Patterson		33:46	3-5	1-3	2-2	+8	2	3	5	2	2	1	2	0	0	9
C. Joseph		16:28	4-8	0-1	0-0	-1	0	3	3	2	0	0	0	0	0	8
T. Ross		07:19	1-3	1-2	0-0	-3	0	1	1	1	0	1	0	0	0	3
J. Johnson		06:05	1-2	0-0	0-0	-3	1	0	1	1	1	0	1	0	1	2
N. Powell	DNP - COACH'S DECISION															
J. Thompson	DNP - COACH'S DECISION															
J. Valanciunas	DNP - COACH'S DECISION															
D. Wright	DNP - COACH'S DECISION															
Total		240	42-78	7-22	14-19		9	26	35	17	16	8	8	3	2	105

TEAM REBS: 6   TOTAL TO: 9

**Kevin Love (25 points) and
Kyrie Irving (23 points) were
dominant in Game 5.**
JOSHUA GUNTER | CLEVELAND.COM

ROUT OF ORDER

CHRIS HAYNES | *cleveland.com*
May 23, 2016

The Cleveland Cavaliers took the slugger moniker back and came out and hit first at the onset of Game 5 of the Eastern Conference Finals.

It was a vicious 37-point opening quarter uppercut that dropped the Toronto Raptors to the hardwood. From there on, the Raptors just staggered in a daze until time expired. Unlike in the sport of boxing, the Raptors couldn't rely on the referees to call the match.

They had to remain on the court and take their beating.

Cleveland is one win away from advancing to the NBA Finals for the second consecutive year after crushing Toronto, 116-78, at Quicken Loans Arena.

Kevin Love, who shot a combined 5-of-23 in Games 3 and 4, broke out of his shooting slump by knocking down his first six field goals and ended with a game-high 25 points on 8-of-10 shooting. He scored inside and out, making three of the four three-pointers he took.

Head coach Tyronn Lue said he spoke to Love the morning of the game and told him to keep shooting. The power forward took heed.

LeBron James registered 23 points, six rebounds and eight assists. Kyrie Irving supplied 23 points.

Cavaliers remind Raptors which team is top seed, taking a 3-2 series lead after colossal 116-78 romp

RAPTORS	POS	MIN	FG-A	3P-A	FT-A	+/-	OFF	DEF	TOT	AST	PF	ST	TO	BS	BA	PTS
D. Carroll	F	26:33	2-7	0-4	1-1	-25	0	2	2	2	2	1	1	0	0	5
L. Scola	F	14:49	3-4	1-2	0-0	-13	0	1	1	3	3	1	0	0	0	7
B. Biyombo	C	21:07	2-3	0-0	3-3	-21	0	4	4	0	3	0	0	1	0	7
D. DeRozan	G	31:09	2-8	0-0	10-12	-32	0	3	3	3	2	2	2	1	0	14
K. Lowry	G	29:11	5-12	1-4	2-6	-25	0	3	3	6	3	1	5	0	2	13
J. Valanciunas		18:27	4-4	0-0	1-2	-17	0	0	0	1	1	0	2	0	0	9
P. Patterson		18:33	1-4	1-3	0-0	-24	0	0	0	0	2	0	2	0	1	3
C. Joseph		10:14	1-5	0-1	1-2	-20	1	1	2	0	1	0	3	0	3	3
T. Ross		21:27	1-4	0-2	1-2	-13	0	2	2	1	5	0	2	0	0	3
J. Johnson		11:04	0-3	0-1	0-0	-3	0	3	3	1	2	1	1	0	0	0
N. Powell		13:26	3-9	0-0	0-0	-1	1	0	1	1	1	1	0	0	0	6
J. Thompson		12:00	1-3	0-0	0-2	+2	3	2	5	1	0	0	0	1	0	2
D. Wright		12:00	2-3	0-0	2-5	+2	0	1	1	0	2	0	0	0	0	6
Total		240	27-69	3-17	21-35		5	22	27	19	25	9	18	3	6	78

TEAM REBS: 11 — TOTAL TO: 19

CAVALIERS	POS	MIN	FG-A	3P-A	FT-A	+/-	OFF	DEF	TOT	AST	PF	ST	TO	BS	BA	PTS
L. James	F	31:30	10-17	2-4	1-3	+31	0	6	6	8	2	2	2	1	0	23
K. Love	F	23:37	8-10	3-4	6-6	+31	2	2	2	1	1	2	2	0	0	25
T. Thompson	C	29:04	2-2	0-0	5-8	+34	5	5	10	0	3	1	0	1	0	9
J. Smith	G	29:07	3-5	1-3	0-0	+34	0	6	6	0	2	4	1	0	0	7
K. Irving	G	27:09	9-17	1-2	4-5	+26	2	1	3	3	3	3	1	1	1	23
I. Shumpert		11:13	0-1	0-1	0-0	+14	0	1	1	0	3	0	1	0	0	0
R. Jefferson		20:02	4-9	1-2	2-2	+4	0	6	6	1	2	0	1	0	2	11
M. Dellavedova		09:16	0-0	0-0	0-0	+11	0	0	0	5	0	0	1	0	0	0
C. Frye		13:13	3-4	1-2	0-0	+9	1	2	3	0	4	0	1	1	0	7
T. Mozgov		12:22	2-2	0-0	0-0	-2	1	6	7	1	2	0	2	0	0	4
J. Jones		12:00	2-3	1-2	0-0	-2	1	0	1	1	1	0	0	0	0	5
M. Williams		12:00	0-4	0-1	0-0	-2	0	0	0	3	0	4	0	0	0	0
D. Jones		09:27	1-3	0-0	0-0	+2	0	3	3	0	0	0	0	0	0	2
Total		240	44-77	10-21	18-24		10	38	48	23	26	11	16	6	3	116

TEAM REBS: 9 — TOTAL TO: 17

J.R. Smith celebrates with LeBron James after winning the Eastern Conference Finals.
GUS CHAN | THE PLAIN DEALER

BEASTS OF THE EAST

CHRIS HAYNES | *cleveland.com*
May 27, 2016

The Cleveland Cavaliers are moving on up to the west side of the conference. A spirited second-quarter combination of lockdown defense and opportunistic offense fueled a 113-87 victory over the Toronto Raptors in Game 6 of the Eastern Conference Finals, advancing the Cavaliers to their second straight NBA Finals.

It was the first time all season that the Cavaliers won in Canada.

LeBron James, who finished with 31 points, 11 rebounds and six assists, will make his sixth connective Finals appearance. Kevin Love will play in his first Finals after registering 20 points, 12 rebounds and four assists.

Kyrie Irving put in 30 points and nine assists.

Cleveland led, 31-25 after one. The team that won the first quarter won every game in this series. Before tipoff, Raptors' faithful were confident this series would extend to seven games.

"LeBron James is obviously a very good game closer, but honestly in this building, anything can happen is how I feel about it," said Raptors season-ticker holder Gavin Hull. "I think we're going back to Cleveland. They can pull it out."

There's only one team going back to Cleveland.

On to the Finals for Cavaliers after (finally) conquering Canada

CAVALIERS	POS	MIN	FG-A	3P-A	FT-A	+/-	OFF	DEF	TOT	AST	PF	ST	TO	BS	BA	PTS
L. James	F	41:15	13-22	3-6	4-7	+22	2	9	11	6	2	1	3	3	0	33
K. Love	F	39:16	5-11	4-8	6-6	+22	0	12	12	4	2	0	0	0	0	20
T. Thompson	C	24:01	1-1	0-0	0-0	+11	2	3	5	0	4	0	1	0	0	2
J. Smith	G	36:27	5-9	5-8	0-0	+22	0	0	1	2	1	0	1	0	0	15
K. Irving	G	39:53	12-24	2-4	4-5	+21	0	4	4	9	1	3	4	1	2	30
C. Frye		14:52	2-3	2-3	0-0	+6	0	1	1	0	4	0	0	1	0	6
R. Jefferson		12:04	1-1	1-1	0-0	+6	0	1	1	0	0	0	0	0	0	3
I. Shumpert		18:12	0-0	0-0	0-0	+14	0	3	3	0	2	1	0	0	0	0
M. Dellavedova		08:44	1-2	0-1	2-3	+4	0	1	1	2	1	0	2	0	0	4
J. Jones		02:38	0-0	0-0	0-0	+1	0	0	0	0	0	0	0	0	0	0
D. Jones		02:38	0-1	0-0	0-0	+1	0	0	0	0	0	0	0	0	0	0
T. Mozgov	DNP - COACH'S DECISION															
M. Williams	DNP - COACH'S DECISION															
Total		240	40-74	17-31	16-21		4	34	38	22	18	6	10	6	2	113

TEAM REBS: 5   TOTAL TO: 11

RAPTORS	POS	MIN	FG-A	3P-A	FT-A	+/-	OFF	DEF	TOT	AST	PF	ST	TO	BS	BA	PTS
D. Carroll	F	28:13	3-9	1-2	0-0	-16	2	4	6	0	3	0	1	0	2	7
L. Scola	F	05:33	0-1	0-1	0-0	-7	0	0	0	0	1	0	1	0	0	0
B. Biyombo	C	26:10	1-4	0-0	2-4	-25	0	9	9	0	2	1	1	1	1	4
D. DeRozan	G	42:14	9-18	0-1	2-2	-24	0	3	3	4	4	0	4	0	1	20
K. Lowry	G	42:19	11-22	6-12	7-7	-30	1	2	3	3	2	0	2	1	2	35
P. Patterson		34:37	3-9	1-5	2-4	-12	0	1	1	2	4	1	1	0	0	9
J. Valanciunas		17:21	3-5	0-0	0-0	+4	4	4	8	1	0	0	0	0	0	6
C. Joseph		13:17	1-3	0-1	0-0	-4	0	0	0	1	2	0	0	0	0	2
T. Ross		07:27	0-1	0-1	0-0	-5	0	0	0	0	0	0	0	0	0	0
J. Johnson		14:55	1-4	0-1	0-0	-8	0	1	1	0	2	0	2	0	0	2
N. Powell		02:38	1-2	0-1	0-0	-1	0	1	1	0	0	1	0	0	0	2
D. Wright		02:38	0-1	0-0	0-0	-1	0	0	0	0	0	0	0	0	0	0
J. Thompson		02:38	0-0	0-0	0-0	-1	0	1	1	0	0	0	0	0	0	0
Total		240	33-79	8-25	13-17		7	26	33	10	19	6	12	2	6	87

TEAM REBS: 9   TOTAL TO: 17

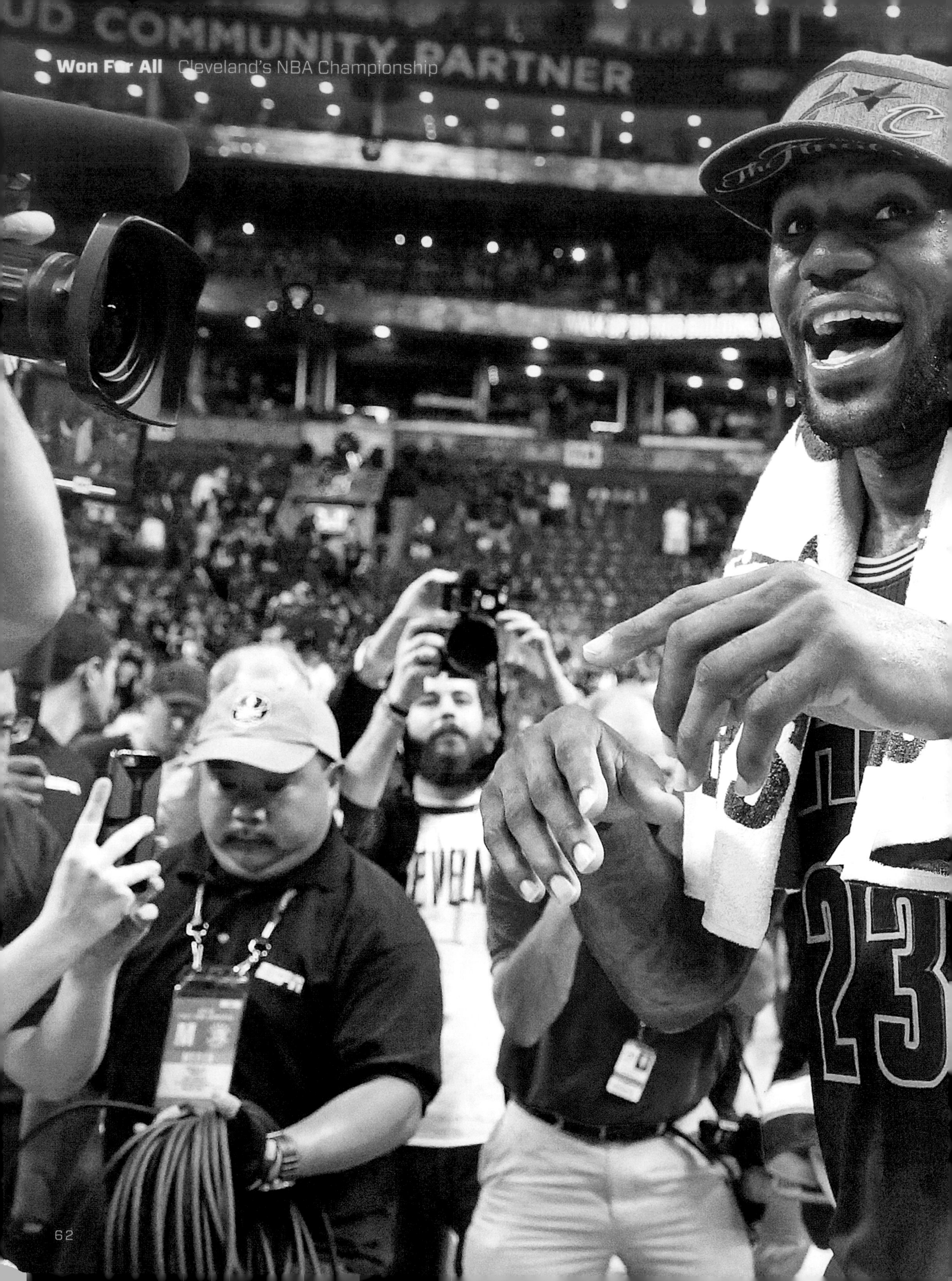
COMMUNITY PARTNER

LeBron James is all smiles after becoming the first player in NBA history to advance to six straight NBA Finals playing for two separate teams (the Heat from 2011-14 and the Cavaliers from 2015-16). THOMAS ONDREY | THE PLAIN DEALER

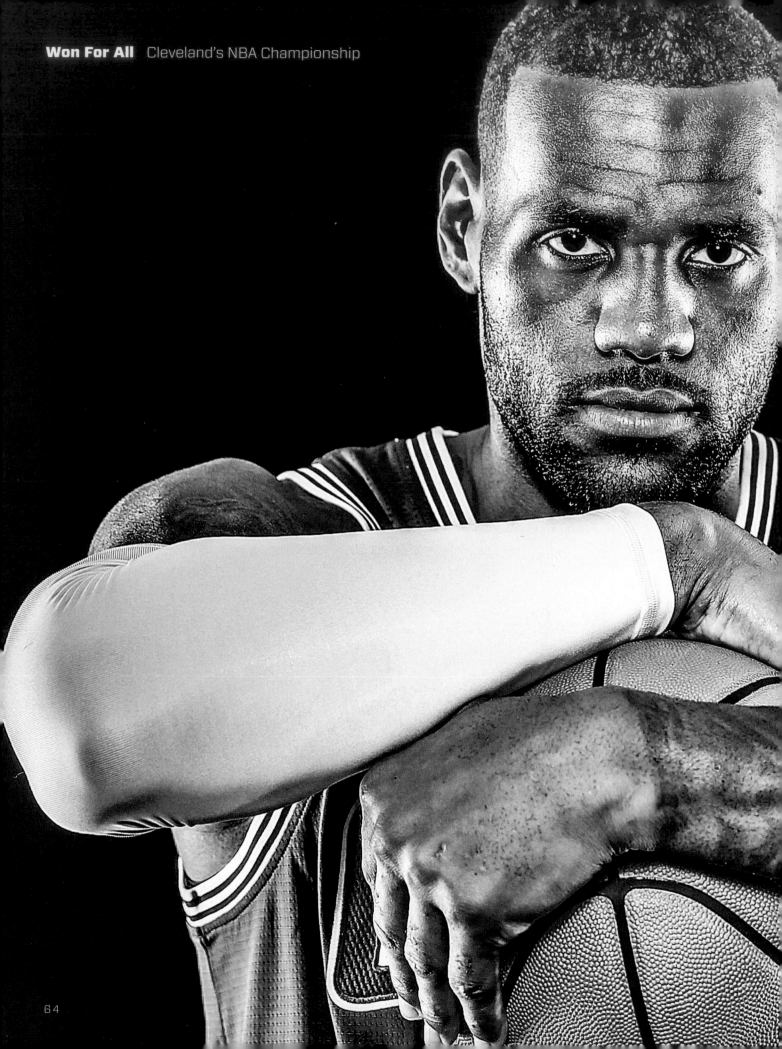

LeBron James

EVERYTHING IS EARNED

LeBron James' sixth consecutive trip to NBA Finals brings 'a different feeling' and greater appreciation

JOE VARDON | *cleveland.com*
May 28, 2016

LeBron James

Through 96 games and 69 wins, 2,264 personal points and a coaching change, two playoff sweeps and a tougher-than-expected Eastern Conference finals, LeBron James fought against a single narrative, a universally shared perception for an entire season. That the Cavaliers were automatically going back to the Finals. ¶ Remember his letter? In Northeast Ohio, nothing is given. Everything is earned. ¶ "We're not entitled to anything," James said in the wee hours of Saturday morning, after he and the Cavs had in fact landed in their second consecutive Finals with a 113-87 romp in Game 6 over the Toronto Raptors. ¶ "We earned the right to be here and represent the Eastern Conference in The Finals," James said. "We work our tails off every single day. We commit to one another and we sacrifice to one another. We're not supposed to be here. We earned our right." ¶ This team has come quite a distance, from early this season when James was ripping teammates for a sense of entitlement to coach Tyronn Lue calling out Kyrie Irving and Kevin Love for caring more about their brands than winning. ¶ The simple fact remains that the Cavs are indeed where everyone thought they would be, the team standing in the East with another Finals on the horizon.

LeBron James throws down a double-pump reverse dunk against Toronto in the Eastern Conference Finals.

JOSHUA GUNTER | CLEVELAND.COM

LeBron James

LeBron James is introduced before facing the Heat at The Q in February. THOMAS ONDREY | THE PLAIN DEALER

It was predicted almost from the moment James strode off the floor for the final time in the 2015 season in Game 6 of the Finals, knowing the Cavs would lose to the Warriors that night and fall two wins shy of the ultimate prize.

Never mind the challenges the team would have to overcome.

Irving and Iman Shumpert missing two months with injuries; Love again needing to feel his way into the flow of the offense; the front office choosing to fire David Blatt and promote Lue to head coach in January even though Cleveland was leading the East.

The Cavs have James. He takes teams to the Finals. That's just how it goes.

The following statistic just rolls off your tongue, as if it were something you mentioned every day when you awake in the morning. It's said with a shrug, like, "Yeah, so?"

James just reached his sixth consecutive Finals.

In an immediate, on-court interview with ESPN's Doris Burke following Game 6, James' voice cracked with emotion on a few occasions going

over some of the same points.

How the Cavs were without Love and Irving for most of the 2015 postseason and virtually all of the Finals because of injury.

In Game 6 against Toronto, James led the Cavs with 33 points, but Irving was right behind with 30 and Love added 20 points and 12 rebounds. To put it in perspective, James scored at least 30 points for the 81st time in his postseason career.

But it seemed so special, so out of the ordinary, because of how consistently Irving and Love have helped James carry the Cavs through the 2016 playoffs.

NBA onlookers were waiting for James to "take over" a playoff game, and what transpired in Toronto counted only because it was the first time this postseason that James went over 30 points.

Irving, averaging 24.3 points for the playoffs (to James' 24.6), and Love, who's contributing 17.3 points and 9.6 rebounds, have essentially shaded the actual impact James has had, especially in the Eastern finals.

LeBron James speaks up in a huddle in a game against the Pacers in February. JOHN KUNTZ | CLEVELAND.COM

In this series, James led the Cavs in scoring (26.0 points) and assists (6.7), and tied for the team lead with Tristan Thompson with 8.5 rebounds. He collected 40 assists compared with 14 turnovers and shot a torrid 62.2 percent from the field.

"We wouldn't be at this point today going to the Finals without those two," James said of Irving and Love, who flanked him at the podium.

Whether or not that's true — would the Cavs be headed to the Finals without Irving or Love — is debatable. They did it last year. But they didn't win — they couldn't, they ran out of bodies against the Warriors.

And that's another reason why this trip to the Finals is different. The Cavs are fully healthy, fully prepared to do what they've never done before, with or without James.

Win a championship.

"We have the right team and we have the right talent," Lue said. "The way we've been playing basketball and trusting one another and coming together as a unit, I think guys understand what we have ahead of us. I'm just happy that everyone gets to enjoy it."

By beating the Raptors Friday, James earned a road win for the 25th consecutive playoff series. According to ESPN, he broke Michael Jordan's old record of 24.

So if the Oklahoma City Thunder completes its upset bid over the Warriors and reaches the Finals, Cleveland would not only have homecourt advantage — it would also have strong odds of winning at least one road game. That's what history tells us.

If Golden State survives and thus holds homecourt over the Cavs, James' track record neutralizes it.

When it comes to narratives surrounding James, it's never just about reaching the Finals. Since he came home from Miami in the summer of 2014, he's been chasing the storybook tale of winning the city's first title since 1964 as the hometown hero.

Last season, James seemed to revel in the win-one-for-Cleveland angle. This year, he's kept his distance from it.

And yet, James, the Cavs, and northeast Ohio are again on the brink. But, this time, it's different.

"I know our city deserves it," James said. "Our fans deserve it. But that gives us no sense of entitlement. We've still got to go out and do it."

LeBron James and Kevin Love celebrate
a semifinal sweep of Atlanta.
THOMAS ONDREY | THE PLAIN DEALER

Kyrie Irving

DUAL
THREAT

After he returned from injury, relentless work habits made Kyrie Irving a perfect complement to James — with either hand

BILL LIVINGSTON | *The Plain Dealer*
April 29, 2016

JOSHUA GUNTER | CLEVELAND.COM

Kyrie Irving

Using both hands with equal ease in basketball is like greatness, which is to say, some men are born to ambidexterity, some men achieve ambidexterity, and some men have ambidexterity thrust upon them. ¶ Count Kyrie Irving among the achievers and thrust upon-ers. ¶ DePaul coach Ray Meyer devised the "Mikan Drill" in the 1940s for the first great center, the Blue Demons' George Mikan. Parked alongside the tiny six-foot-wide lane of the era, the 6-10 Mikan scored at will with either hand, in college and in the early years of the NBA, once he got the hang of it. ¶ The drill is now standard for big men, but point guards also use it to help them finish with a basket and not a miss. ¶ In the Mikan Drill, players shoot both left-handed and right-handed layups, reverse layups and hooks without stopping or letting the ball bounce to the floor. It obviously requires stamina. It also develops touch. ¶ On some shots, the ball doesn't just kiss the glass, but almost reaches basketball's sky, bussing the top of the 18-inch-high white square above the 10-foot-high rim. ¶ Irving did the Mikan Drill. To the max. ¶ "The angles of the backboard — I have to use them. I'm not going over the top of anybody," said Irving.

Kyrie Irving

Kyrie Irving
scores and is
fouled against the
Magic in January.
CHUCK CROW
THE PLAIN DEALER

Kyrie Irving

Kyrie Irving is introduced as a starter for the first time this season on December 20. GUS CHAN | THE PLAIN DEALER

"When I was seven or eight years old, I was doing the Mikan Drill and my dad had me start doing reverses (layups). My nose started bleeding. I was so dizzy I almost passed out."

LeBron James, who also did the Mikan Drill as a boy, is still clearly Closer No. 1. But Irving is 1A.

Against Detroit, Irving became the only teammate of James' other than Miami's Dwyane Wade in the Heat's loss in the 2011 NBA Finals to outscore James in a playoff series.

Irving averaged 27.5 points in the four-game sweep of the Pistons to James' 22.8.

The endowments of greatness

Teammates and fans know how hard Irving worked to get back into the lineup after undergoing surgery for a season-ending broken kneecap in 2015.

The loneliness of the long-distance shooter is a basketball stereotype. We do not accord flashy drives and showy dunks the respect of

Kyrie Irving

such solitary dedication, although that was the case with Irving.

Scoring around the basket is more popularly considered a result of explosive jumping and power. These are the LeBron traits, encoded in the DNA of the 6-8 superstar, refined in practice, yet still inherent in a way with which no 6-2, comparatively gravity-bound player, such as Irving, will identify.

Irving has an explosive first step and is a long strider. He can get to the rim in one dribble from near the 3-point arc. That's the LeBron increment in his game.

It all starts to become patently unfair with a body spin by Irving that makes the defender's gyroscope go all the way to "tilt," like a pinball machine pushed too far back in the day.

The hard work of greatness

The rest of Irving's finishing is made of parts patiently shaped on the lathe of practice, practice and more practice.

Kyrie Irving

"I don't believe in ball-handling gurus," Irving said, when asked if he had any instructor as a boy besides his father, Drederick. "I didn't do anything like close one eye, pick up the basketball, pick up a tennis ball, or dribble two balls at once. It's a cliche, but I'd be out there alone, playing against (invisible) guys, coming up with things."

In the poetry in motion to which basketball is sometimes compared, a hesitation move is like the caesura, or break, in a line of poetry. Something emotional and dramatic often follows in a poem.

After Irving's hesitation dribble in basketball, what follows can be a burst past a lulled defender and a jack-knifing reverse layup or an off-balance shot with whichever hand can thread the ball through the clutter more effectively.

Sometimes, the final move to the rim comes on a high, hard dribble that creates the basketball equivalent of an arm-over pass rushing move in football.

At the rim, Irving's Mikan Drill mastery of angles and ball rotation convince you that fairy tales are true and that gold really can be spun from straw.

An additional element in Irving's ball-handling is a cross-over dribble that is close to an optical illusion. In the context of a great cross-over dribbler, such as that of Hall of Famer Allen Iverson or Irving, normal visual experience is almost useless. The ball suddenly and simply is in the other hand without even the courtesy of a cry of "Abracadabra!"

What this means is that the prestidigitation and legerdemain and other words that amount to hocus-pocus are the result of perspiration, not inspiration.

By the way, foul him and pay the price. Irving ranked 10th in the NBA this season, making 88.5 percent of his free throws.

Sniper

"We have designated snipers," James said of the Cavaliers' 3-point-centric offense. "I am not one of them. I'm more of a tank."

Irving has better inside-out versatility than anyone on the Cavs' roster, and that includes James.

Now, the bad news for Atlanta, the Cavs' next playoff opponent: Irving has regained his 3-point touch.

He shot 84 for 261, a sub-par 32.2 percent, in the 53 games he played in the regular season after recovering from knee surgery. Against Detroit in the Cavs' hard-won four-game sweep, Irving made 16 of 34, 47.1 percent.

"He's usually around 38 or 39 percent. When you're coming back from an injury after missing games, it takes time to get your legs under you. I'm glad he's getting his rhythm at the perfect time," said Cavs coach Tyronn Lue.

Daggers

Irving swished a shot from half-court at the end of the third quarter of the Cavs' 100-98 victory in the elimination game. No Piston thought he would shoot it from there. But he did.

Talk about finishing!

It broke a 78-78 tie. A shot only has to be released before the game or shot clock buzzer. It still counts if it plummets into the net after nothing but zeroes flash on the clock. With Irving, it ain't over even when it's over.

It wasn't J.R. Smith's heroic shot clock beater against blanket coverage in the final minute of the fourth game, but the only more extensive range than that of J.R. is probably where the deer and antelope play.

Irving's catch-and-shoot splashdown 3-pointer from the corner against the shot clock in the third game of the series came on a play that started with 0.7 of a second on the shot clock. It expanded a five-point lead. It was the result of a brilliant out of bounds play drawn up by Lue.

Matthew Dellavedova threw an inbound pass from the corner on the baseline on a shallow angle to the opposite corner, where Irving caught it in rhythm. The Pistons' Tobias Harris, guarding Irving near the top of the foul circle, was slowed by James' back screen. No one rotated toward Irving because James then cut toward Delly's side of the court, drawing everyone except Harris to him.

Irving raced to the open corner and caught the pass. Harris closed frantically and challenged just ... barely ... too ... late. When the ball landed in the net on Irving's fadeaway three, it took the game with it.

His step-back 3-pointer is to spatial clearance from a defender what a bargain basement sale is to merchandise clearance from the shelves.

When the ball sticks

Critics will always hound Irving for monopolizing the ball. But in the Detroit series, he had 19 assists to six turnovers, a ratio of better than three to one. James' totals were 27 assists and 13 turnovers, a ratio of better than two to one. By one count, though, 17 of James' assists were for 3-pointers.

Isolation sets were part of the game plan against the Pistons when James or Irving had a match-up they could exploit, according to Lue. The Cavs used them heavily as the offense stagnated at the end of the fourth game.

Irving said of the strategy, "At the end of the day, we have two of the best closers in the game playing on the same team."

Still, there was a moment late in the close-out game, with James dribbling outside the arc in what was to be a 1-4 isolation set. James pointed to the corner, where he wanted Irving to set up for a possible drive-and-kick 3-pointer.

Irving rolled his eyes in exasperation, then moved to the corner.

Perhaps it was petulant. But go easy on the theme of individualism at the expense of collective purpose. Irving had put in the work.

Kyrie Irving

**Irving hugs
LeBron James
after a playoff win
over the Pistons.**
GUS CHAN
THE PLAIN DEALER

Kevin Love

BIG MAN OUTSIDE

Kevin Love is a stretch
power forward who is
lethal as a 3-point shooter,
but he still finds ways to
wreak havoc inside

BILL LIVINGSTON | *The Plain Dealer*
May 13, 2016

Big men dreamed in the past of doing the flashy things that were the exclusive property of quick, darting guards. ¶ They are hard dreams to give up today, too. ¶ Just Tuesday night (midway through the Cavs' Eastern Conference Finals series with the Raptors), Dwight Howard said on "Inside the NBA" on the TNT Network that he would love to be able to bring the ball up, dribble between his legs, and go to the rim. "But I'm dependent on my teammates [to provide the ball]," he said. ¶ Such fantasies were spawned by 6-9 point guard Magic Johnson. They were poorly imitated by, among others, Kobe Bryant's father, Joe, and a 7-4 center from the University of Virginia, Ralph Sampson, who was the prize of the draft in the early 1980s almost to the extent that LeBron James would be years later. ¶ The whole psychological twist of bigs wanting to play small was jokingly called — because of the player's extraordinary height, even by NBA standards, and out of body fantasies — "Ralph Sampson's Disease." ¶ In today's NBA, the "stretch" big shoots 3-pointers from the arc. This is ironic in that the 3-pointer's philosophical intent was to bring the small outside shooter back to a game in which height usually made might.

Kevin Love sinks a wide-open 3-pointer against the Clippers in January.

JOSHUA GUNTER | CLEVELAND.COM

Kevin Love

Kevin Love and LeBron James share a laugh late in Game 1 of the Eastern Conference Finals. JOHN KUNTZ | CLEVELAND.COM

But how many big defenders are going to contest 6-10 Cavalier Kevin Love's 3-point shot, when a strong challenge can open the driving lanes to the basket for dunks by LeBron James?

In the playoffs, Love's scoring and rebounding have been impressive. His size and his ball-handling limitations, compared to the multi-faceted James and point guard Kyrie Irving, have destined him to be the third member of the Cavs' Big Three.

Currently, Love is the antithesis of the traditional post-up big man. If you want to find where his points are coming from now, look to the horizon. Love's play in the playoffs reveals a statistical gulf between hot shooting on the arc and cold shooting inside it. Against Atlanta's athletic big men, Love was 19-for-40 on threes, nearly 50 percent. But he was a paltry 4-for-31 inside the arc, 12.9 percent.

In eight playoff games, Love is 28-of-63, a robust 44 percent, on 3-pointers and 20-for-69, an anemic 29 percent, inside the line.

It is fine for a big to hit threes at a clip only smalls once were thought capable of maintaining. It is quite another for a big to play small

Kevin Love

in the paint. Unfortunate as the metaphor might be, if this were the weekend warrior game of paintball, Love would be a Jackson Pollock canvas, splattered by the Hawks.

Rebounds and hard hats

Love might be a stretch 4 (power forward) as far as his scoring goes, but he easily leads the Cavs in playoff rebounding with 100, 75 on the defensive end.

James at 70 and Tristan Thompson with 66, with a stunning 40 offensive boards, are next.

Love played at UCLA, and his uncle Mike Love was a founding member of the seminal 1960s California band, the Beach Boys. It would be easy to caricature Kevin as a cars and surf kind of guy, except that his father, Stan, was a journeyman player in the ABA and NBA, who

The crowd reacts to a Kevin Love 3-pointer in Game 5 of the Eastern Conference Finals. JOHN KUNTZ | CLEVELAND.COM

schooled him in such Old School skills as the bank shot.

As he showed in the Detroit series, which was actually the much tougher of the two sweeps, Love was willing to make the hustle plays that often separate victory from defeat.

In Atlanta, he was smashed down in Game 3 in a hard collision with Al Horford, which referees completely ignored, that should have been a charge.

The slump was the exception

"(Love) missed some shots he's accustomed to making," said James. "He was able to make up for it defensively, in rebounding, and he shot the 3-ball well. We're not concerned with what he didn't do in the paint. He did the opposite of me.

"I lived in the paint and didn't make the three."

"They were physical with him," said Cavs coach Tyronn Lue of the Hawks' strategy. "They fronted him. They double-teamed him. So we spread the floor with LeBron and Kyrie, and he got some good looks on threes."

The Hawks' defensive strategy of packing the paint to obstruct James and Irving left them vulnerable outside. The result resembled giving a long acupuncture treatment to Achilles' heel.

For his part, Love vowed that his time as a pincushion in the paint is over.

"As (Atlanta's) Kent Bazemore said, they dared me to shoot (the 3-pointer)," Love said. "(Al) Horford and Millsap were great on defense. It's not something that's going to happen again."

"I believe Kevin is a top 10 player in the league, the one we all hoped we'd see," said Lue.

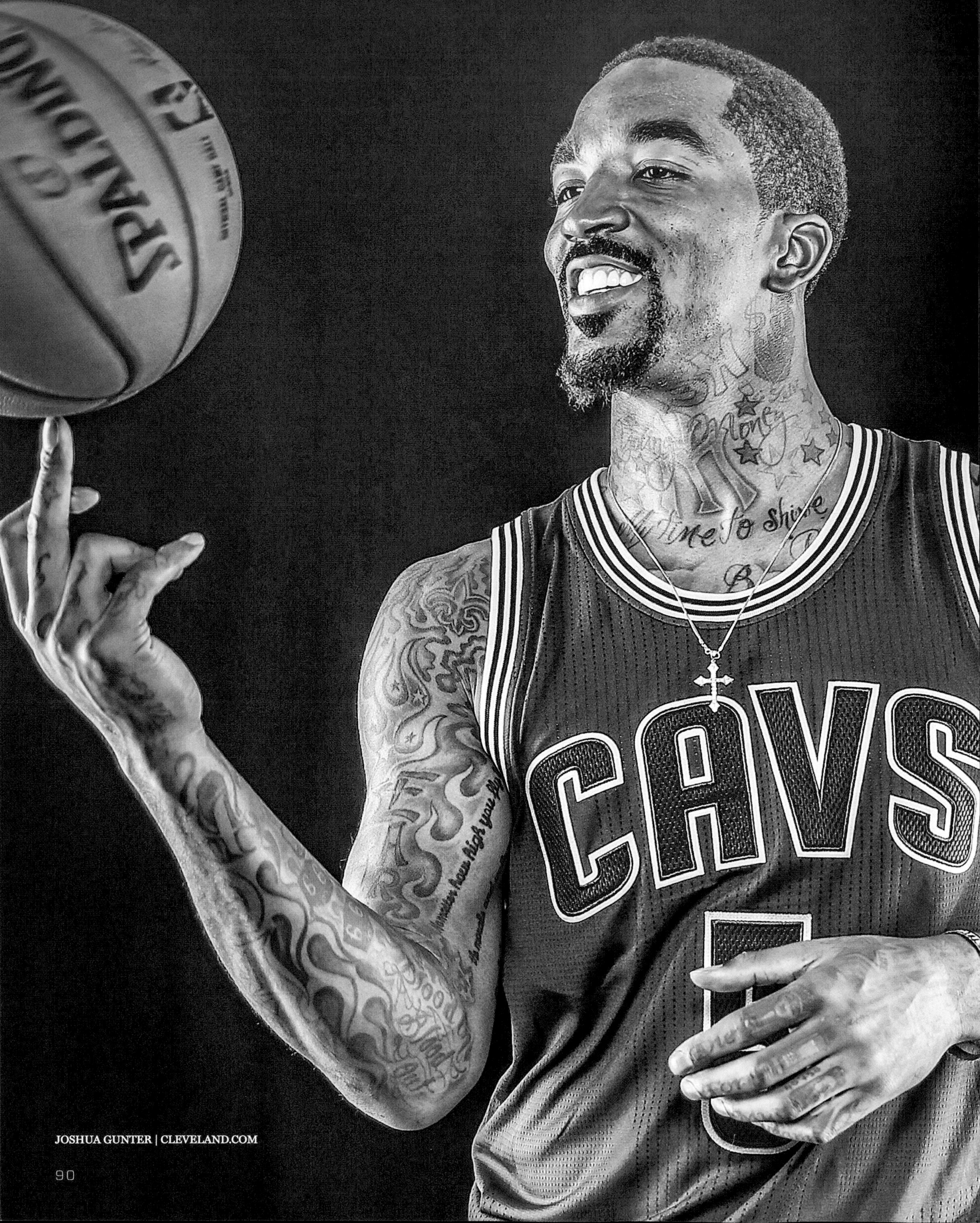

JOSHUA GUNTER | CLEVELAND.COM

THE MAN WITH THE ULTRA GREEN LIGHT

BILL LIVINGSTON | *The Plain Dealer*
May 5, 2016

U sually, basketball coaches preach that swift passing minimizes defensive clutter and tidies up shooting sight lines.

From this ball movement comes open jump shots and proof that cleanliness is next to godliness. Or something like that.

Then there is J.R Smith.

When he gets hot, Smith cuts through the bonds of the defense as easily as the fellow who sliced the thick knot with his sword back in the very old days. That was Alexander the Great, who really didn't "untie" the Gordian knot, but cheated with the blade.

Still, the reward was the promise of being king of Asia, so here's to independent thought by both Alexander and Smith, who thinks he can make any shot, from anywhere.

"It's sort of boring when you're wide open. People expect you to make it," said Smith after the first game of the Atlanta playoff sweep last season.

Smith is on his way to putting the nickname "Swish" back in good standing here after the rapid decline of the Indians' injury-plagued Nick Swisher.

Smith started out, however, going to the NBA straight from high school, hoping to be another LeBron James. "That didn't work out very well for me," he said.

What did work out was a jump-shooting game with the elevation and strength to get off shots while doing 180-degree spins in mid-air, while falling backward, while falling out of bounds, and while imitating a video game.

Smith's affinity for contested shots has kept his career 3-point percentage below the top tier of shooters. His average is 37.5 percent overall, but 40 percent this season. In the current playoff season, he is a preposterous 28 of 53, 52.8 percent.

Asked if he would like, just on a one-day fling, to be Smith, a grinning James said, "That's almost a trick question. You mean where you can just shoot any shot that you want? Yeah."

James added, "J.R. is the only one who has the ultra green light. Coach says, 'Shoot it, J.R.. Shoot it, shoot it. When you're open, when you're not close enough, just shoot it.'"

The Cavs are playing the best and most interdependent basketball in the nine seasons of James' career in which he has played here. A championship is the goal. James is the "King," but a kingdom in Asia is not on his bucket list or that of any other Cavalier. But if it were, "J.R. Buckets" might be someone's new nickname.

J.R. Smith's NBA career has been star-crossed, but the Cavs only ask one thing of him: Knock down open shots

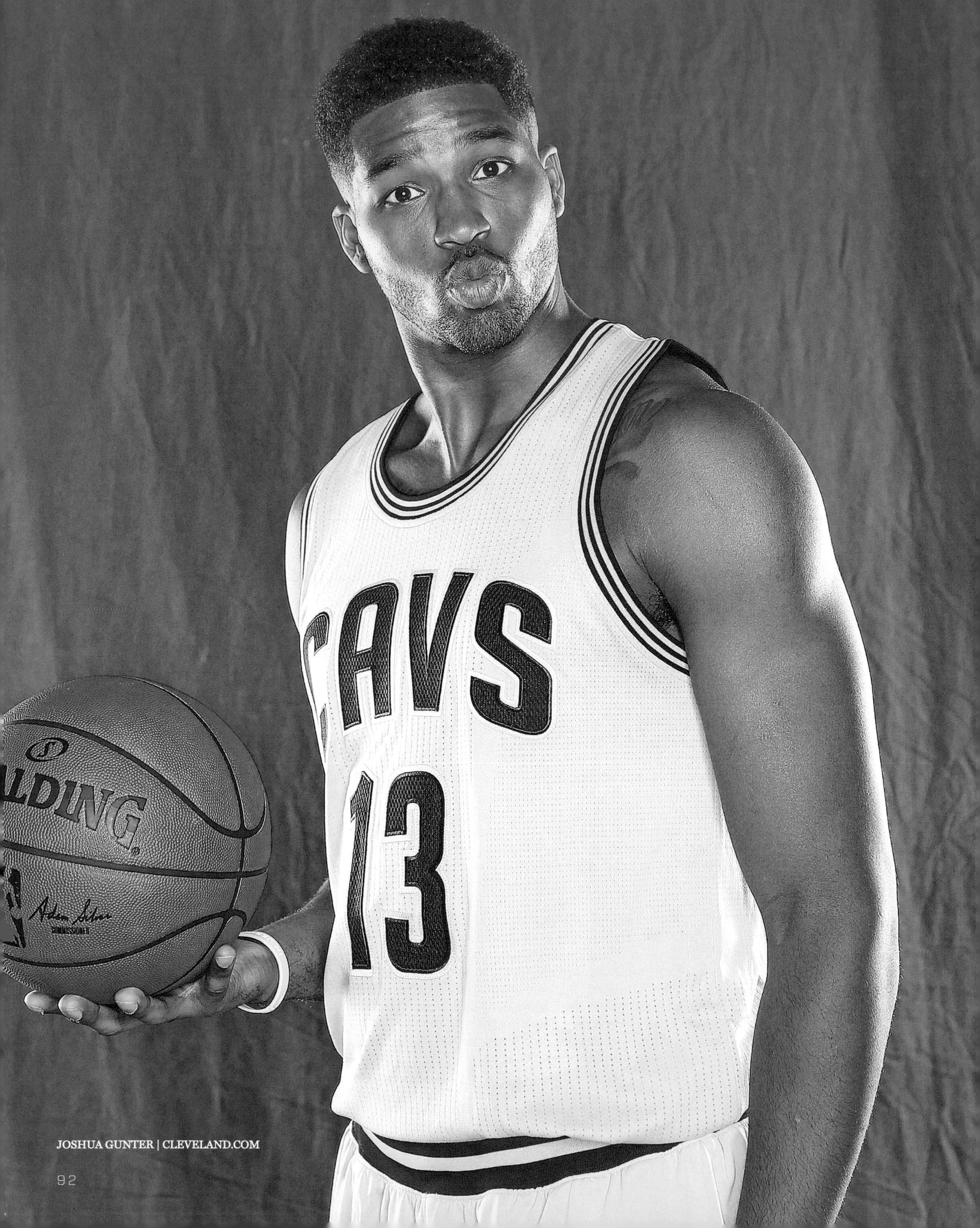

JOSHUA GUNTER | CLEVELAND.COM

REJECTING THE BIGGEST SHOTS

BILL LIVINGSTON | *The Plain Dealer*
May 10, 2016

W hen the Cleveland Cavaliers are engaged and almost enraged on defense, they can run opponents off the 3-point line. They can "blitz" the ball-handler and make the pick-and-roll seem more like the hope-and-pray.

The flaw is that they cannot protect the rim as well as they can the arc. This has been the case ever since center Timofey Mozgov was sent to the gulag at the end of the bench for poor play. The need today is for a big man who is light enough on his feet to guard smaller men on the perimeter on switches and still do yeoman work at traditional tasks of rebounding and shot-blocking.

One out of two on those traditional duties might not be enough as the playoffs continue in several days with the Eastern Conference finals against either Miami or Toronto. But one out of two is what the Cavs get with Tristan Thompson.

LeBron James called Thompson "an offensive rebounding machine" during the injury-plagued Cavs' limp to the NBA Finals last season. Thompson's ability to give the Cavs extra possessions with his rebounding is a tremendous asset. He is 6-9, but has the wingspan of a man 7-2.

His shot-blocking is not underrated. It's barely rated. He averages only slightly more than one every two games this season.

Perhaps, to paraphrase Spencer Tracy's merry (and sexist by today's standards) appraisal of Katharine Hepburn as "choice" in "Pat and Mike," all we can say is, "There's not much meat, but what there is, is cherce."

In the Atlanta series, according to a Cavs source who watched every game twice, when Thompson contested the Hawks' shots, they made only nine of 41 overall, 22 percent. Paul Millsap, their top inside scorer, was 5-of-24, 20.8 percent. When Dennis Schroder was speeding past either Kyrie Irving or Matthew Dellavedova with equal ease in Sunday's final second-round series game against Atlanta, it was Thompson who knocked aside the Atlanta guard's driving layup with 63 seconds to play and the Cavs leading, 98-97.

In the final two seconds, with the Cavs leading 100-99, Thompson loomed in front of the rim and Schroder, who had to pick up his dribble after Irving's side-swipe at the ball. As Schroder pump-faked, James came from the blind side to tie him up. The Cavs won the jump ball, the game and the series.

It's not all blocked shots or even alterations of them. Hesitations, which, like altered shots, are never accounted for in the box score, help win games too.

Thompson allowed his sharp-shooting teammates room to roam with his fearsome inside presence

DRIVING FORCE

The Cavs' roster was deep on talent, experience necessary to make a championship run

JOSHUA GUNTER | CLEVELAND.COM

JOSHUA GUNTER | CLEVELAND.COM

JOSHUA GUNTER | CLEVELAND.COM

Matthew Dellavedova

76 games	**9** blocks
1,867 minutes	**40.5**% field goal shooting
569 points	
337 assists	**41.0**% 3-point shooting
162 rebounds	
44 steals	

Timofey Mozgov

76 games	**57** blocks
1,326 minutes	**56.5**% field goal shooting
475 points	
33 assists	**14.3**% 3-point shooting
337 rebounds	
22 steals	

Richard Jefferson

74 games	**14** blocks
1,326 minutes	**45.8**% field goal shooting
410 points	
59 assists	**38.2**% 3-point shooting
128 rebounds	
33 steals	

JOSHUA GUNTER | CLEVELAND.COM

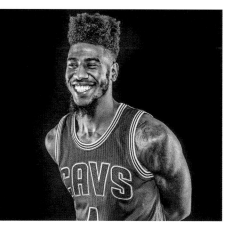

JOSHUA GUNTER | CLEVELAND.COM

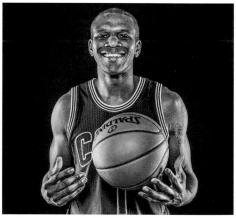

JOSHUA GUNTER | CLEVELAND.COM

Mo Williams

41 games	**5** blocks
748 minutes	**43.7**% field goal shooting
338 points	
98 assists	**35.3**% 3-point shooting
72 rebounds	
14 steals	

Iman Shumpert

54 games	**19** blocks
1,316 minutes	**37.4**% field goal shooting
311 points	
92 assists	**29.5**% 3-point shooting
203 rebounds	
54 steals	

James Jones

48 games	**10** blocks
463 minutes	**40.8**% field goal shooting
178 points	
14 assists	**39.4**% 3-point shooting
50 rebounds	
11 steals	

GUS CHAN | THE PLAIN DEALER

Channing Frye

26 games
446 minutes
196 points
93 assists
93 rebounds
8 steals

8 blocks
44.1% field goal shooting
37.7% 3-point shooting

JOSHUA GUNTER | CLEVELAND.COM

Jordan McRae

15 games
113 minutes
62 points
15 assists
12 rebounds
0 steals

1 block
44.2% field goal shooting
63.6% 3-point shooting

GUS CHAN | THE PLAIN DEALER

Dahntay Jones

1 game
42 minutes
13 points
2 assists
5 rebounds
1 steal

2 blocks
42.9% field goal shooting
50.0% 3-point shooting

Joe Harris

Harris was traded to Orlando for luxury tax considerations, along with a 2017 second-round pick in exchange for a 2020 second-round pick, on Jan 13.

Anderson Varejao

After 12 seasons with the Cavs, the center was traded to Portland in a three-team deal with Orlando. He was released and signed with the Warriors on Feb. 21.

Jared Cunningham

Cunningham was traded to Orlando with a draft pick as part of the 3-team deal that shipped Varejao and brought Channing Frye to Cleveland on Feb. 18.

JOSHUA GUNTER | CLEVELAND.COM

Sasha Kaun

24 games
95 minutes
22 points
3 assists
26 rebounds
4 steals

5 blocks
52.9% field goal shooting
(3-point shooting N/A)

Tristan Thomnpson, James Jones, Iman Shumpert, LeBron James and Matthew Dellavedova look to the sidelines during a game against the Nuggets at The Q. JOSHUA GUNTER | CLEVELAND.COM

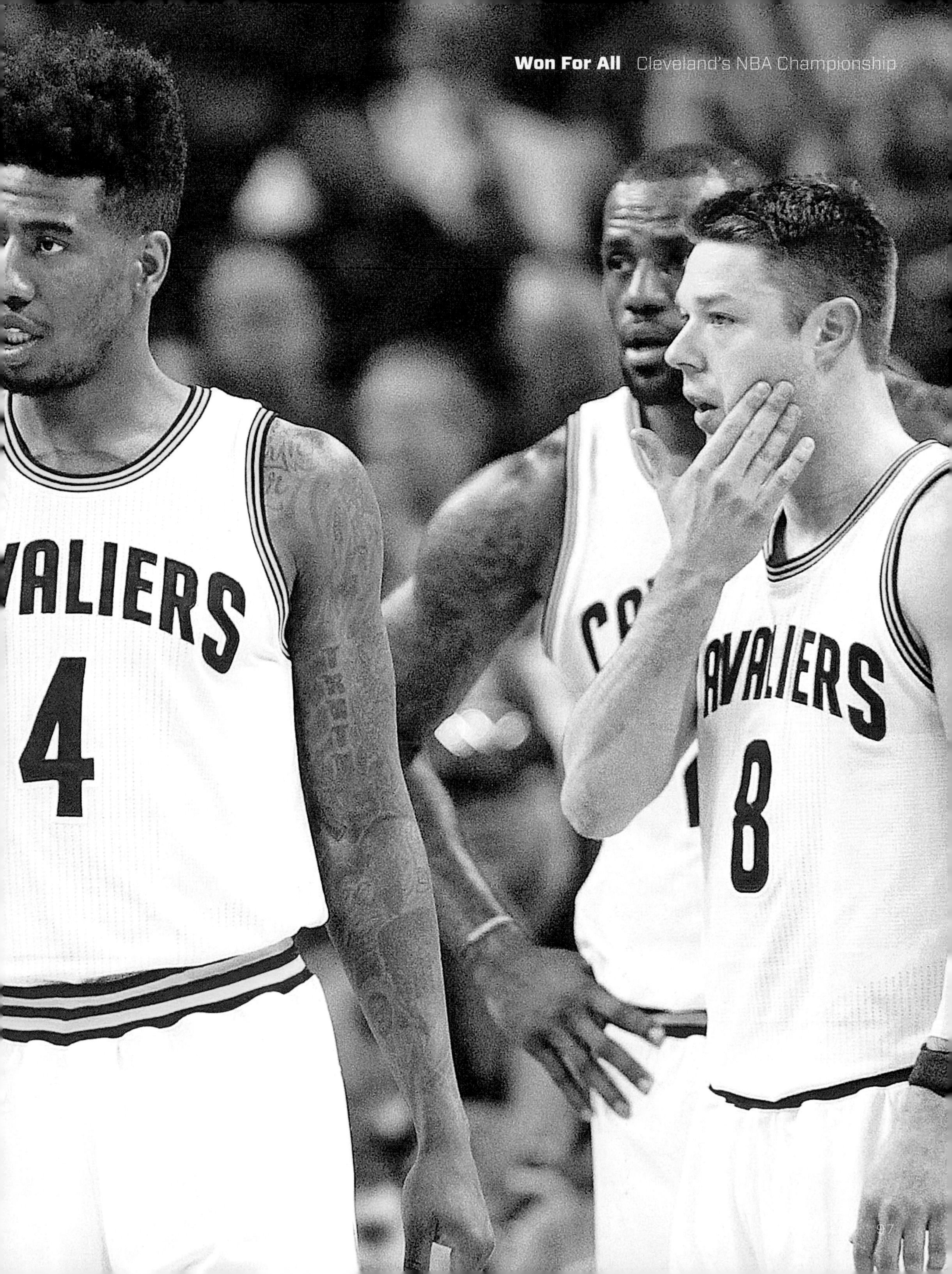
VALIERS
4
CAVALIERS
8

THE BEST TO EVER PLAY IN CLEVELAND

Terry Pluto | *The Plain Dealer*
May 30, 2016

Cavaliers heading into NBA Finals with the greatest team in franchise history

I have never seen a better Cleveland Cavaliers team than this one.

There have been several times during the playoffs when that thought crossed my mind. But it really hit home during their final two victories of the Eastern Conference Finals.

This is the best Cavs team ... ever.

Not the best in terms of record.

But the best when it comes to talent.

The best when it comes to having a future Hall of Famer who truly knows how to lead a team to the NBA Finals.

The best when it comes to combining LeBron James with two young stars — but not rookies. I'm talking about Kyrie Irving and Kevin Love.

This is the best team in Cavs history, and I have seen them all since the franchise began in 1970.

Are they good enough to knock off Golden State?

Not so sure about that. But they certainly are in better position than a year ago when they lost to the Warriors in the Finals.

LeBron James is 31. Kevin Love is 27. Tristan Thompson is 25. Kyrie Irving is 24. J.R. Smith is 31. All of those players are in their prime.

Among the others who are regular rotation members, only Richard Jefferson (36) and Channing Frye (33) would be considered past their peak years — but they still can play.

The 6-foot-11 Frye will probably be throwing in 3-pointers at the age of 90. Jefferson is in amazing condition for a 15-year veteran. The ages also indicate the Cavs should be able to contend for the next few years. That's especially true in the Eastern Conference.

Never before has a Cavs team advanced this deep in the playoffs with this combination of talent, experience and health. It still may not be enough. Golden State is scary and has the heart and rings of a champion.

In his "Coming Home" essay in Sports Illustrated, James wrote: "In Northeast Ohio, nothing is given, everything is earned."

That's so true.

And never have the Cavs had a team in a better position to go out and earn the franchise's first title.

Andre Iguodala keeps the ball away from Kyrie Irving in Game 1.
GUS CHAN
THE PLAIN DEALER

SUB NATION

TERRY PLUTO | *The Plain Dealer*
June 3, 2016

F or the Cleveland Cavaliers and their fans, this one hurt..

Imagine going into the opening game of the 2016 NBA Finals knowing that the Golden State star guards would score 20 points.

That's 20 points COMBINED for Stephen Curry and Klay Thompson.

That's 20 almost agonizing points on 8-of-27 shooting.

You'd have to like the Cavs chances.

Final Score: Golden State 104, Cavs 89.

Ouch!

Even worse, the Cavs came from 13-points behind early in the game to take a 68-67 lead in the third quarter ...

And they were outscored, 37-21, in the rest of the game.

It would be one thing if Thompson and Curry were splashing jumpers from Golden Gate Bridge. Instead, they were banging shots off these Oracle Arena rims that they love so much.

And the Cavs still lost.

The Warriors are the defending champs. They were 39-2 in this building during the regular season, and they are now 10-1 in the playoffs.

Now you know why Steve Kerr believes his team has an advantage.

Warriors'
bench
outscores
Cleveland's
by 35 in
Game 1
rout

Golden State's Andre Iguodala throws down two of his 12 points during the Warriors' 104-89 win Thursday. MARCIO JOSE SANCHEZ / ASSOCIATED PRESS

GOLD BLOODED
Warriors' stars don't shine but the defending champs' bench guts the Cavaliers

CHRIS HAYNES | chaynes@cleveland.com

The rematch of all rematches finally began Thursday evening at Oracle Arena, but it produced the same results. ¶ In Game 1 of the NBA Finals, the Golden State Warriors defeated the Cleveland Cavaliers, 104-89, in large part because of the Warriors' bench production. The defending champions' reserves outscored the Cavaliers' bench, 45-10. ¶ It is now the sixth consecutive time the Warriors have beaten the Cavaliers, dating back to last June. ¶ The point of emphasis for the Cavaliers was containing Stephen Curry. ¶ "Everyone's going to have a role trying to guard Curry. He's a tough player and we know he makes this team go," Cavaliers coach Tyronn Lue said. "... Everybody has to be locked in and focused on Steph."

Pluto: With Warriors dominating at home, series could be hard to watch. **C3** | **Livingston:** Even superstars need a little help. **C3**

Cavaliers		POS	MIN	FG-A	3P-A	FT-A	+/-	OFF	DEF	TOT	AST	PF	ST	TO	BS	BA	PTS
L. James		F	40:53	9-21	2-4	3-4	-10	4	8	12	9	2	2	4	1	1	23
K. Love		F	37:21	7-17	2-5	1-1	-9	2	11	13	2	2	1	4	0	0	17
T. Thompson		C	31:00	5-11	0-0	0-0	-5	6	6	12	0	3	0	0	1	2	10
J. Smith		G	36:16	1-3	1-3	0-0	-14	0	1	1	1	5	0	1	0	0	3
K. Irving		G	37:39	7-22	1-4	11-12	-10	1	2	3	4	2	3	3	0	1	26
C. Frye			07:10	0-1	0-1	2-2	+4	0	1	1	0	0	0	0	0	0	2
I. Shumpert			16:47	1-1	1-1	0-0	-15	0	1	1	0	2	0	1	0	0	3
R. Jefferson			12:24	1-3	0-1	1-1	-10	2	0	2	0	0	0	0	0	0	3
M. Dellavedova			10:54	1-3	0-1	0-0	-19	0	0	0	1	1	0	1	0	0	2
D. Jones			02:24	0-0	0-0	0-0	+2	0	0	0	0	0	0	0	0	0	0
M. Williams			02:24	0-2	0-1	0-0	+2	0	0	0	0	0	1	0	0	0	0
T. Mozgov			02:24	0-0	0-0	0-0	+2	0	2	2	0	0	0	0	1	0	0
J. Jones			02:24	0-0	0-0	0-0	+2	0	0	0	0	0	0	0	0	0	0
Total			240	32-84	7-21	18-20		15	32	47	17	17	7	15	4	4	89

TEAM REBS: 9   TOTAL TO: 17

On the ball
Cavs' turnovers give Warriors extra chances
Turnovers/points off TO

Q1			
Q1	CLE	5/11	3/4	GSW
Q2	CLE	4/4	1/0	GSW
Q3	CLE	3/3	2/5	GSW
Q4	CLE	5/7	3/3	GSW

see CAVALIERS | C4

CLEVELAND.COM/CAVS

Warriors		POS	MIN	FG-A	3P-A	FT-A	+/-	OFF	DEF	TOT	AST	PF	ST	TO	BS	BA	PTS
H. Barnes		F	30:11	6-10	0-2	1-1	+8	0	1	1	1	1	0	0	1	13
D. Green		F	40:17	5-11	2-6	4-4	+18	0	11	11	7	1	4	3	1	0	16
A. Bogut		C	15:25	5-7	0-0	0-0	-8	2	1	3	2	2	0	0	0	0	10
K. Thompson		G	24:23	4-12	1-5	0-1	+5	0	5	5	2	3	0	2	1	9
S. Curry		G	35:54	4-15	3-8	0-0	0	1	4	5	6	2	0	5	0	0	11
A. Iguodala			35:52	5-9	2-4	0-0	+22	3	4	7	6	1	1	0	1	0	12
F. Ezeli			10:29	1-4	0-0	0-0	+3	1	2	3	0	1	1	0	0	1	2
S. Livingston			26:34	8-10	0-0	4-4	+20	1	3	4	3	2	0	0	0	0	20
A. Varejao			03:19	0-1	0-0	0-0	+4	1	0	1	1	1	0	0	0	0	0
L. Barbosa			11:25	5-5	1-1	0-0	+14	0	1	1	1	0	1	0	0	0	11
I. Clark			02:38	0-0	0-0	0-0	-2	0	0	0	0	0	1	0	0	0
M. Speights			02:01	0-2	0-1	0-0	-2	0	0	0	1	0	0	0	0	0
B. Rush			01:32	0-1	0-0	0-0	-2	0	0	0	0	0	0	0	0	0
Total			240	43-87	9-27	9-10		9	32	41	29	16	9	9	4	4	104

TEAM REBS: 2   TOTAL TO: 9

Draymond Green knocks down a 3-pointer against J.R. Smith in Game 2.

GREEN'S DAY

TERRY PLUTO | *The Plain Dealer*
June 5, 2016

Golden State's Draymond Green, left, and Klay Thompson reject a shot by the Cavs' LeBron James in the third quarter on Sunday in Oakland.

Heads hanging ... Fingers pointing ... Frustration oozing ...

That what it was like for the Cleveland Cavaliers in the middle of the third quarter during the 110-77 loss to Golden State on Sunday night.

Before the game, Cavs coach Tyronn Lue said: "We're a very confident group. So our guys are not taken aback or shaken because it's just one loss on their home floor."

Well, make it two ... as in two decisive, confidence-rattling losses.

"They did what we were supposed to do," Lue said after the game. "They won their two at home. We have to do the same on our home court."

Fact is, the Cavs are behind 0-2 in the best-of-seven NBA Finals. Since 2009, only two of 56 teams in that position in a series came back to win. Oklahoma City did it in 2012, Memphis in 2013.

Yes, it's that bad because the Cavs weren't even close to winning the opener (104-89). Then they disintegrated and embarrassed themselves in this game. It was unwatchable.

The Cavs have been among the best offensive teams in the NBA this season. But they have scored 89 and 77 points in these two games, shooting 37 percent from the field.

> Draymond Green scores 28 as Warriors coast to 2-0 series lead

CAVALIERS	POS	MIN	FG-A	3P-A	FT-A	+/-	OFF	DEF	TOT	AST	PF	ST	TO	BS	BA	PTS
L. James	F	33:38	7-17	1-5	4-4	-20	0	8	8	9	3	4	7	1	2	19
K. Love	F	20:46	2-7	1-4	0-0	-8	0	3	3	0	0	1	1	0	2	5
T. Thompson	C	19:13	3-8	0-0	2-2	-13	3	2	5	0	4	1	0	0	2	8
J. Smith	G	33:24	2-6	1-4	0-2	-22	1	1	2	2	3	2	1	0	0	5
K. Irving	G	33:06	5-14	0-3	0-0	-26	1	2	3	1	1	3	3	0	2	10
R. Jefferson		26:01	4-6	0-0	4-6	-13	2	3	5	0	2	1	1	1	1	12
M. Dellavedova		16:42	2-9	1-2	2-2	-14	0	1	1	2	1	0	0	0	0	7
I. Shumpert		19:53	1-3	1-3	0-0	-14	0	1	1	0	1	0	1	0	0	3
C. Frye		03:52	0-1	0-0	0-0	-3	0	1	1	0	0	0	0	1	0	0
T. Mozgov		12:00	1-3	0-0	3-4	-13	2	1	3	0	3	1	2	0	0	5
J. Jones		08:37	0-0	0-0	0-2	-4	0	2	2	1	0	0	0	0	0	0
M. Williams		08:11	0-3	0-2	0-0	-6	0	0	0	1	0	2	1	0	0	0
D. Jones		04:37	1-2	0-0	1-2	-3	0	0	0	0	0	0	0	0	0	3
Total		240	28-79	5-23	16-24		9	25	34	15	19	15	17	3	9	77

TEAM REBS: 13 TOTAL TO: 18

WARRIORS	POS	MIN	FG-A	3P-A	FT-A	+/-	OFF	DEF	TOT	AST	PF	ST	TO	BS	BA	PTS
H. Barnes	F	34:30	2-7	0-2	1-2	+11	1	4	5	1	0	1	3	1	1	5
D. Green	F	33:52	11-20	5-8	1-1	+20	1	6	7	5	2	1	1	0	1	28
A. Bogut	C	14:57	1-4	0-0	0-0	+10	3	3	6	0	4	2	2	5	0	2
K. Thompson	G	31:29	6-13	4-8	1-1	+23	0	2	2	5	1	2	4	0	1	17
S. Curry	G	24:43	7-11	4-8	0-0	+25	1	8	9	4	4	0	4	1	0	18
A. Iguodala		28:22	3-6	0-2	1-3	+28	3	2	5	3	1	0	2	1	0	7
S. Livingston		24:08	3-4	0-0	1-1	+12	0	2	2	5	2	0	1	1	0	7
F. Ezeli		10:58	2-3	0-0	2-2	+2	1	1	2	1	1	1	1	0	0	6
L. Barbosa		17:39	5-7	0-2	0-0	+21	1	2	3	1	1	1	0	0	0	10
I. Clark		07:37	3-4	1-2	0-0	+6	1	2	3	1	2	1	0	1	0	7
B. Rush		07:08	0-0	0-0	0-0	+4	0	2	2	0	1	0	1	0	0	0
M. Speights		04:37	1-2	1-1	0-0	+3	0	0	0	0	2	0	0	0	0	3
A. Varejao		DNP - COACH'S DECISION														
Total		240	44-81	15-33	7-10		12	34	46	26	20	7	20	9	3	110

TEAM REBS: 16 TOTAL TO: 21

LeBron James watches as the play continues after being knocked to the floor in the first half of Game 2 of the NBA Finals.
THOMAS ONDREY | THE PLAIN DEALER

A determined Kyrie Irving scored
30 points in Game 3.

JOSHUA GUNTER | CLEVELAND.COM

LORDS OF THE 'LAND

CHRIS HAYNES | *cleveland.com*
June 8, 2016

All the Cleveland Cavaliers needed was a little home cooking.

The Golden State Warriors found out that playing at The Q was mighty different from playing at Oracle. On Wednesday night in Game 3 of the NBA Finals, the Cavaliers crushed the Warriors, 120-90 to claim their first victory of the series.

It ended a seven-game losing streak to the Warriors.

LeBron James delivered his second 30-point outing of the postseason -- 32 to combine with 11 rebounds and six assists. Kyrie Irving went for 30 points and eight assists.

Kevin Love was unable to go because the team wouldn't clear him due to the concussion he suffered on Sunday.

"We know Kevin wants to play, he's eager to play. He's frustrated that he's not able to play," Cavaliers coach Tyronn Lue said. "But that's the protocol and that's how we're trying to protect our players nowadays in the NBA. That's just what it is. So someone else has to step up right now."

Richard Jefferson entered the lineup and Cleveland jumped out on Golden State as if they stole something. Irving was in attack mode. He had Stephen Curry backpedalling hard.

At The Q, Cavs look very much alive in Game 3 blowout

THE PLAIN DEALER

nbafinals
THURSDAY, JUNE 9, 2016 | SECTION C | 8 PAGES

LeBron James completes a reverse slam against the Golden State Warriors as the Cavaliers take control of Game 3 in the first half at The Q.

ROLE REVERSAL
Cavaliers come alive to thump Warriors and resuscitate hopes for an NBA championship

CLEVELAND.COM/CAVS

WARRIORS							REBOUNDS									
	POS	MIN	FG-A	3P-A	FT-A	+/-	OFF	DEF	TOT	AST	PF	ST	TO	BS	BA	PTS
H. Barnes	F	33:22	7-11	2-5	2-3	-24	1	7	8	3	2	0	1	0	0	18
D. Green	F	35:56	2-8	0-4	2-4	-15	1	6	7	7	4	0	2	1	1	6
A. Bogut	C	12:01	2-6	0-1	0-0	-21	2	0	2	0	2	0	1	1	0	4
K. Thompson	G	30:39	4-13	1-7	1-3	-27	1	1	2	1	1	1	2	0	0	10
S. Curry	G	30:59	6-13	3-9	4-4	-22	1	0	1	3	4	2	6	0	0	19
A. Iguodala		28:25	5-7	1-2	0-0	-10	0	2	2	0	0	0	1	0	0	11
F. Ezeli		02:48	0-1	0-0	0-0	-4	0	0	0	0	0	0	0	0	0	0
S. Livingston		19:46	2-3	0-0	1-2	-3	1	5	6	3	2	0	3	1	0	5
M. Speights		07:55	1-4	1-2	2-2	-6	0	1	1	0	1	0	0	0	0	5
L. Barbosa		16:42	2-5	0-1	4-6	-4	0	0	0	2	3	2	0	1	0	8
A. Varejao		09:56	0-1	0-0	1-2	-2	1	1	2	2	3	0	1	0	0	1
B. Rush		05:53	0-1	0-0	0-0	-7	0	1	1	0	0	0	0	0	0	0
I. Clark		05:39	1-3	1-2	0-0	-5	0	0	0	1	1	0	1	0	0	3
Total		240	32-76	9-33	17-26		8	24	32	21	23	5	18	4	4	90

TEAM REBS: 9   **TOTAL TO: 18**

CAVALIERS							REBOUNDS									
	POS	MIN	FG-A	3P-A	FT-A	+/-	OFF	DEF	TOT	AST	PF	ST	TO	BS	BA	PTS
R. Jefferson	F	33:13	4-7	1-3	0-0	+11	3	5	8	2	3	2	1	0	0	9
L. James	F	40:04	14-26	1-2	3-5	+24	2	9	11	6	2	1	5	2	0	32
T. Thompson	C	31:01	5-6	0-0	4-5	+21	7	6	13	2	2	0	0	0	0	14
J. Smith	G	37:59	7-13	5-10	1-2	+33	0	4	4	1	1	3	0	0	1	20
K. Irving	G	36:36	12-25	3-7	3-3	+24	1	3	4	8	4	1	2	0	2	30
I. Shumpert		17:39	1-5	1-2	0-0	+9	2	3	5	1	3	0	2	0	1	3
T. Mozgov		06:37	1-2	0-0	0-0	+11	1	1	2	0	4	1	2	0	0	2
C. Frye		12:21	0-0	0-0	0-0	+4	0	0	0	3	0	0	1	0	0	0
M. Dellavedova		07:39	1-2	0-0	0-0	-10	1	1	0	1	0	0	0	0	0	2
M. Williams		04:38	1-2	1-1	0-0	+5	0	2	2	0	1	0	1	0	0	3
D. Jones		04:38	0-1	0-0	0-0	+5	0	1	1	0	1	0	0	0	0	0
J. Jones		04:38	0-0	0-0	1-2	+5	2	0	2	0	0	0	0	0	0	1
J. McRae		02:57	2-2	0-0	0-0	+8	0	1	1	0	0	0	0	0	0	4
Total		240	48-91	12-25	12-17		17	35	52	23	25	8	13	3	4	120

TEAM REBS: 8   **TOTAL TO: 14**

#ALLFORONE

BRAD DAUGHERTY	ZYDRUNAS ILGAUSKAS
43	11

LOUDVILLE

| CAVS | 77 | 20 | 2:48 | 3Q | WARRIORS | 59 | FG% | 45 | FOULS | 4 | TOL: 20s | FULL 2 | 10:54 PM |

In the second half, LeBron James emphatically slams home two of his game-high 32 points in Game 3.

JOSHUA GUNTER | CLEVELAND.COM

Kyrie Irving
punches the
padding under the
basket after missing
a layup in Game 4.

JOHN KUNTZ
CLEVELAND.COM

Warriors 108, Cavaliers 97 Game 4

ALL IN TROUBLE

CHRIS HAYNES | *cleveland.com*
June 10, 2016

Series turns ugly as physical Warriors push Cavs to bring of elimination

The Cleveland Cavaliers are officially facing a death sentence.

After Friday night's 108-97 Game 4 triumph, the Golden State Warriors are one win — presumably in Game 5 in Oakland — away from repeating.

Stephen Curry broke out of a shooting slump to torture the Cavaliers for a game-high 38 points while sinking seven three-pointers. Klay Thompson also had a good evening with 25 points and splashing in four threes. The Warriors tied a Finals record with 17 threes, with four from Harrison Barnes and two from Andre Iguodala.

This game — until the fourth quarter — was what most expected for the entire series. Thrilling, physical and back-and-forth with 14 lead changes. Neither really separated until the Cavaliers went nearly seven minutes without a basket early in the final period.

The home team had a six-point lead entering the second half, but the ball movement that kept the Warriors off-balance disappeared as LeBron James and Kyrie Irving traded futile drives for much of the half.

The two combined for 49 of the team's 81 shots — making their 59 combined points far less efficient than it seems on first glance.

WARRIORS			FIELD GOALS				REBOUNDS									
	POS	MIN	FG-A	3P-A	FT-A	+/-	OFF	DEF	TOT	AST	PF	ST	TO	BS	BA	PTS
H. Barnes	F	40:10	5-11	4-5	0-0	+6	3	5	8	2	1	1	0	0	1	14
D. Green	F	42:14	2-9	0-4	5-8	+15	1	11	12	4	4	2	3	3	0	9
A. Bogut	C	10:01	0-0	0-0	0-0	0	1	0	1	1	1	0	1	0	0	0
K. Thompson	G	39:23	7-14	4-9	7-7	+11	0	4	4	1	2	1	1	1	0	25
S. Curry	G	39:39	11-25	7-13	9-10	+11	3	2	5	6	2	3	2	0	2	38
A. Iguodala		37:08	4-12	2-5	0-0	+15	2	4	6	7	3	1	1	1	2	10
S. Livingston		18:34	3-8	0-0	2-2	+3	1	2	3	1	3	0	0	0	1	8
J. McAdoo		07:24	1-1	0-0	0-0	+3	0	1	1	1	2	0	0	0	0	2
F. Ezeli		01:19	0-0	0-0	0-2	-3	0	0	0	0	1	0	0	0	0	0
A. Varejao		04:02	0-1	0-0	2-2	-1	3	0	3	0	2	0	0	0	0	2
M. Speights		00:06	0-0	0-0	0-0	0	0	0	0	0	0	0	0	0	0	0
L. Barbosa		DNP - COACH'S DECISION														
I. Clark		DNP - COACH'S DECISION														
Total		240	33-81	17-36	25-31		14	29	43	23	22	7	8	6	6	108

TEAM REBS: 11   TOTAL TO: 9

CAVALIERS			FIELD GOALS				REBOUNDS									
	POS	MIN	FG-A	3P-A	FT-A	+/-	OFF	DEF	TOT	AST	PF	ST	TO	BS	BA	PTS
R. Jefferson	F	24:53	1-2	0-0	1-2	-5	2	4	6	0	6	0	2	0	0	3
L. James	F	45:34	11-21	1-5	2-4	-13	4	9	13	9	4	2	7	3	2	25
T. Thompson	C	28:34	5-7	0-0	0-5	-10	6	1	7	0	3	0	0	1	1	10
J. Smith	G	43:24	3-10	2-8	2-2	-12	0	2	2	1	5	0	0	0	1	10
K. Irving	G	43:22	14-28	2-6	4-5	-12	1	3	4	4	2	3	1	1	2	34
K. Love		25:00	3-6	1-2	4-6	-5	1	4	5	0	1	0	0	1	0	11
I. Shumpert		14:37	1-5	0-3	0-0	-1	1	0	1	0	0	1	0	0	0	2
M. Dellavedova		04:43	0-1	0-1	2-2	0	1	0	1	1	1	1	0	0	0	0
C. Frye		09:45	0-1	0-0	0-0	-2	0	1	1	0	2	0	1	0	1	0
D. Jones		00:08	0-0	0-0	0-0	0	0	0	0	0	0	0	0	0	0	0
J. Jones		DNP - COACH'S DECISION														
T. Mozgov		DNP - COACH'S DECISION														
M. Williams		DNP - COACH'S DECISION														
Total		240	38-81	6-25	15-26		16	24	40	15	24	5	11	6	6	97

TEAM REBS: 14   TOTAL TO: 11

Stephen Curry gestures toward Lebron
James during the fourth quarter of Game 4.

JOSHUA GUNTER | CLEVELAND.COM

Kyrie Irving and LeBron James share a hug after combining for 82 points in Game 5.

THOMAS ONDREY
THE PLAIN DEALER

Cavaliers 112, Warriors 97 Game 5

ALIVE IN FIVE

CHRIS HAYNES | *cleveland.com*
June 13, 2016

LeBron James throws down two of his 41 points Monday during Game 5 of the NBA Finals in Oakland. James also had 16 rebounds and seven assists.
BOB DONNAN | USA TODAY SPORTS

THE KING AND KY

LeBron and Irving combine for 82 points as Cavs stave off elimination

Terry Pluto

There will be another game for the Cavaliers, and that says a lot about this team. ¶ Take a bow, LeBron James. ¶ And Kyrie Irving. ¶ You two became the first players in NBA Finals history to score at least 40 points in the same game as the Cavs kept their playoff hopes alive with a 112-97 victory over Golden State at Oracle Arena Monday night. ¶ Each put 41 points next to their names. ¶ It started with James. ¶ He had the stars. ¶ It's the scowl that screamed, "Not tonight," to the screaming Warriors fans wearing "STRENGTH IN NUMBERS" T-shirts. ¶ And it continued with Irving, who played a gritty, determined game as if to prove a point to his critics...by scoring lots and lots of points. ¶ Games like this are a reminder of the kind of big-time talent Irving possesses. ¶ Irving went right at Stephen Curry, daring the MVP to try and stop him. All the pressure Irving put on Curry seemed to wear down the Golden State star.

Analysis: Cavs stars explode, giving team another chance in Finals. **C2** | **Livingston:** James hushes the boo-birds with dominance. **C5**

SEE PLUTO | **C4**

James, Irving each turn in 41 points as Cavs get back in series with road blowout

The NBA Finals aren't over yet. It's because of Kyrie Irving and LeBron James.

The two went for a ridiculous 41 points each to propel the Cleveland Cavaliers to a 112-97 victory over Golden State on Monday night at Oracle Arena. It narrows The Finals to a 3-2 Warriors lead with Game 6 coming Thursday at The Q.

Irving knocked down huge basket after huge basket in an 12-point fourth quarter. It was just a continuation of a brilliant night -- 17-of-24 from the floor, including 5-of-7 from deep.

James pulled down 16 boards, distributed seven assists and connected on three triples. His 25 points in the first half calmed the Cavs through the energy provided by Warriors fans determined to see a clinching victory.

Kevin Love returned to the starting lineup after coming off the bench in Game 4, but was only able to provide two points and three rebounds in 34 minutes. It didn't matter all that much because the Warriors' offense disappeared in the fourth quarter, posting just one point in the last 6:39.

An Irving three-pointer put the Cavaliers up 13 with 4:41 left to play. Oracle became uncharacteristically mute.

CAVALIERS	POS	MIN	FG-A	3P-A	FT-A	+/-	OFF	DEF	TOT	AST	PF	ST	TO	BS	BA	PTS
L. James	F	42:38	16-30	4-8	5-8	+13	4	12	16	7	1	3	2	3	1	41
K. Love	F	32:53	1-5	0-3	0-0	+18	0	3	3	1	4	0	2	2	1	2
T. Thompson	C	41:32	1-3	0-0	4-10	+11	3	12	15	0	1	1	0	2	1	6
J. Smith	G	30:43	3-9	1-2	3-3	+11	1	1	2	1	5	1	1	0	3	10
K. Irving	G	39:47	17-24	5-7	2-2	+20	0	3	3	6	4	2	4	1	1	41
R. Jefferson		14:18	4-6	0-1	0-0	+7	0	1	1	0	1	3	3	0	1	8
M. Dellavedova		03:28	0-2	0-2	0-0	-5	0	0	0	0	3	0	2	0	1	0
I. Shumpert		25:41	2-4	0-1	0-0	+6	0	1	1	0	0	1	1	2	0	4
M. Williams		03:23	0-0	0-0	0-0	-3	0	0	0	0	1	0	1	0	0	0
T. Mozgov		01:52	0-0	0-0	0-0	-1	0	0	0	0	0	1	0	0	0	0
D. Jones		01:52	0-0	0-0	0-0	-1	0	0	0	0	1	0	0	0	0	0
J. Jones		01:52	0-0	0-0	0-0	-1	0	0	0	0	0	0	0	0	0	0
C. Frye	DNP - COACH'S DECISION															
Total		240	44-83	10-24	14-23		8	33	41	15	22	11	16	10	9	112

TEAM REBS: 11   TOTAL TO: 16

WARRIORS	POS	MIN	FG-A	3P-A	FT-A	+/-	OFF	DEF	TOT	AST	PF	ST	TO	BS	BA	PTS
A. Iguodala	F	41:02	6-13	1-4	2-2	-13	4	7	11	6	0	2	3	0	3	15
H. Barnes	F	37:54	2-14	1-6	0-2	-6	1	4	5	1	1	1	0	1	1	5
A. Bogut	C	07:35	0-0	0-0	0-0	-6	1	2	3	0	4	0	2	3	0	0
K. Thompson	G	40:31	11-20	6-11	9-9	-21	0	3	3	1	2	0	1	0	2	37
S. Curry	G	40:07	8-21	5-14	4-4	-6	2	5	7	4	2	0	4	3	3	25
F. Ezeli		09:31	1-3	0-0	0-0	+4	2	1	3	0	2	0	0	1	1	2
J. McAdoo		07:37	0-0	0-0	0-0	-10	0	2	2	0	3	0	0	0	0	0
L. Barbosa		09:53	1-3	1-2	0-0	-5	0	0	0	3	0	2	0	0	3	3
S. Livingston		21:13	3-7	0-1	1-1	-16	1	3	4	3	1	1	3	0	0	7
A. Varejao		08:36	0-0	0-0	3-8	+5	1	0	1	1	0	0	0	0	0	3
M. Speights		11:20	0-6	0-3	0-0	+1	1	2	3	2	2	1	2	0	0	0
B. Rush		04:41	0-1	0-1	0-0	-2	0	1	1	0	1	1	0	1	0	0
D. Green	NWT - NBA SUSPENSION															
Total		240	32-88	14-42	19-26		13	30	43	18	21	6	17	9	10	97

TEAM REBS: 16   TOTAL TO: 17

115

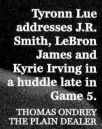

Tyronn Lue
addresses J.R.
Smith, LeBron
James and
Kyrie Irving in
a huddle late in
Game 5.
THOMAS ONDREY
THE PLAIN DEALER

117

LeBron James throws down a dunk in the first half of Game 6.

JOHN KUNTZ
CLEVELAND.COM

Cavaliers 115, Warriors 101 Game 6

BEAST UNLEASHED

CHRIS HAYNES | *cleveland.com*
June 16, 2016

When the Cavaliers took the floor for Game 6 of the NBA Finals, the theme music of WWE's wresting superstar Undertaker was playing in the background.

The fans had on black T-shirts with "CLE" on the front. Some team was going to be laid to rest, and it was the Warriors who met their makers on Thursday night as the Cavaliers evened the series at three games apiece with a 115-101 win.

"When they had a chance to celebrate in our locker room, that left a bitter taste in our mouth," Cavs coach Tyronn Luc said. "So, we've got to come out tonight and be very prepared and ready to fight and play like we've been playing in games 3 and 5."

His team and LeBron James followed suit. The four-time MVP supplied 41 points for the second straight game, eight rebounds and 11 assists in 43 minutes.

"When you don't want to go home and your back's against the wall, he seems to perform better," Lue said.

The Warriors' first basket came with 6:55 left in the first quarter — a period in which Cleveland's lead went from 11, to 17 all the way up to 22.

James lights up Warriors for 41 — again — as Cavs rally from 3-1 down to force NBA Finals to a Game 7

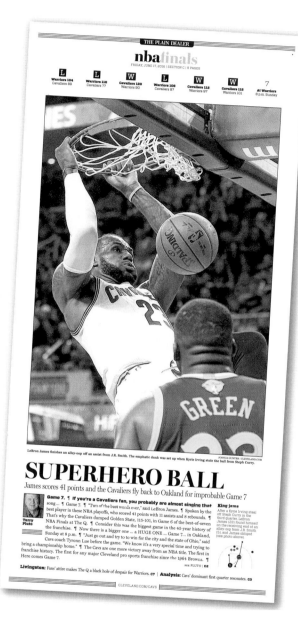

THE PLAIN DEALER

nba finals
FRIDAY, JUNE 17, 2016 | SECTION C | 8 PAGES

L	L	W	L	W	W	7
Warriors 104 Cavaliers 89	**Warriors 110** Cavaliers 77	**Cavaliers 120** Warriors 90	**Warriors 108** Cavaliers 97	**Cavaliers 112** Warriors 97	**Cavaliers 115** Warriors 101	**At Warriors** 8 p.m. Sunday

LeBron James finishes an alley-oop off an assist from J.R. Smith. The emphatic dunk was set up when Kyrie Irving stole the ball from Steph Curry.

JOSHUA GUNTER / CLEVELAND.COM

SUPERHERO BALL

James scores 41 points and the Cavaliers fly back to Oakland for improbable Game 7

Game 7. ¶ If you're a Cavaliers fan, you probably are almost singing that song ... ¶ Game 7. ¶ "Two of the best words ever," said LeBron James. ¶ Spoken by the best player in these NBA playoffs, who scored 41 points with 11 assists and 8 rebounds. ¶ That's why the Cavaliers dumped Golden State, 115-101, in Game 6 of the best-of-seven NBA Finals at The Q. ¶ Consider this was the biggest game in the 45-year history of the franchise. ¶ Now there is a bigger one ... a HUGE ONE ... Game 7... in Oakland, Sunday at 8 p.m. ¶ "Just go out and try to win for the city and the state of Ohio," said Cavs coach Tyronn Lue before the game. "We know it's a very special time and trying to bring a championship home." ¶ The Cavs are one more victory away from an NBA title. The first in franchise history. The first for any major Cleveland pro sports franchise since the 1964 Browns. ¶ Here comes Game 7.

Terry Pluto

King James
After a Kyrie Irving steal off Steph Curry in the third quarter, LeBron James (23) found himself on the receiving end of an alley-oop from J.R. Smith (5), and James obliged (see photo above).

NBA PLUTO, C2

Livingston: Fans' attire makes The Q a black hole of despair for Warriors. **C7** | **Analysis:** Cavs' dominant first quarter resonates. **C3**

CLEVELAND.COM/CAVS

WARRIORS	POS	MIN	FG-A	3P-A	FT-A	+/-	OFF	DEF	TOT	AST	PF	ST	TO	BS	BA	PTS
H. Barnes	F	16:26	0-8	0-5	0-0	-20	0	2	2	0	2	0	0	1	1	0
A. Iguodala	F	30:19	2-5	1-3	0-2	-25	2	2	4	3	2	0	1	0	0	5
D. Green	C	40:44	3-7	0-2	2-2	-12	1	9	10	6	5	1	1	1	2	8
K. Thompson	G	38:05	9-21	3-10	4-7	-22	2	1	3	1	2	2	4	1	3	25
S. Curry	G	35:14	8-20	6-13	8-9	-11	0	2	2	1	6	1	4	0	1	30
F. Ezeli		14:42	2-5	0-0	0-0	-17	3	1	4	1	3	0	1	0	0	4
S. Livingston		21:26	1-6	0-0	1-2	-10	0	4	4	3	3	0	1	0	0	3
L. Barbosa		18:42	4-6	2-3	4-5	+8	1	1	2	2	0	0	1	0	0	14
A. Varejao		06:49	0-0	0-0	0-0	+8	0	1	1	1	2	1	1	0	0	0
B. Rush		08:28	0-0	0-0	1-2	+18	0	1	1	0	0	0	0	0	0	1
J. McAdoo		03:23	1-1	0-0	0-0	+3	0	1	1	0	0	0	0	0	0	2
I. Clark		03:23	1-1	1-1	0-0	+3	0	0	0	1	0	0	0	0	0	3
M. Speights		02:19	2-2	2-2	0-0	+7	0	1	1	0	0	0	0	0	0	6
Total		240	33-82	15-39	20-29		9	26	35	19	25	5	14	3	7	101

TEAM REBS: 13 TOTAL TO: 14

CAVALIERS	POS	MIN	FG-A	3P-A	FT-A	+/-	OFF	DEF	TOT	AST	PF	ST	TO	BS	BA	PTS
L. James	F	42:35	16-27	3-6	6-8	+26	2	6	8	11	3	4	1	3	0	41
K. Love	F	11:55	1-3	1-2	4-6	-6	1	2	3	2	3	0	1	0	1	7
T. Thompson	C	42:38	6-6	0-0	3-4	+32	2	14	16	3	4	0	3	0	0	15
J. Smith	G	40:22	5-11	4-10	0-0	+20	0	4	4	3	5	3	0	1	1	14
K. Irving	G	39:14	7-18	2-5	7-7	+25	1	3	4	3	2	2	3	2	1	23
R. Jefferson		31:52	1-3	0-1	1-2	+15	2	4	6	1	3	2	1	0	0	3
M. Williams		05:40	2-2	0-0	0-0	-2	0	1	1	0	0	0	0	0	0	4
I. Shumpert		14:10	0-2	0-2	0-0	-13	0	1	1	4	0	1	0	0	0	0
D. Jones		04:37	1-1	0-0	3-3	-6	0	1	1	0	0	0	1	0	0	5
T. Mozgov		02:19	0-1	0-0	0-0	-7	0	1	1	0	0	0	0	0	0	0
J. Jones		02:19	0-1	0-1	0-0	-7	0	0	0	1	0	0	0	0	0	0
M. Dellavedova		02:19	1-2	0-0	1-2	-7	0	0	0	1	0	0	0	0	0	3
C. Frye		DNP - COACH'S DECISION														
Total		240	40-77	10-27	25-32		8	37	45	24	25	12	10	7	3	115

TEAM REBS: 9 TOTAL TO: 12

LeBron James
stares down
Steph Curry
after blocking
his shot in the
second half of
Game 6.

JOSHUA GUNTER
CLEVELAND.COM

Kyrie Irving shoots over Anderson Varejao in Game 7.

PROMISED 'LAND

CHRIS HAYNES | *cleveland.com*

June 19, 2016

W t happened on the road at Oracle Arena. It's not a dream. Most considered it an impossible feat. No team in 32 tries had ever come all the way back from being down 3-1 to win the NBA Finals.

Now, it's 1-32.

The Cleveland Cavaliers completed the unimaginable on Sunday nigh, a 93-89 Game 7 victory over the Golden State Warriors to win the franchise's first NBA championship.

LeBron James has delivered Cleveland's first professional championship in 52 years. He led all players in this series in points, assists, steals and blocks. He registered 27 points, 11 rebounds and 11 assists Sunday to earn the Finals MVP award. But he couldn't have done this without Kyrie Irving, who played big to the tune of 26 points and six assists.

The teams traded fruitless possessions over nearly three minutes until Irving delivered the deciding blow.

With 53 seconds remaining, Irving had the Warriors' Stephen Curry on him in an isolation set. Irving yo-yo'ed the ball and hit a killer stepback to put his team up, 92-89. The Cavaliers' bench leaped for joy.

Irving's shot clinches title; Cavs complete comeback as James is named MVP

CAVALIERS	POS	MIN	FG-A	3P-A	FT-A	+/-	OFF	DEF	TOT	AST	PF	ST	TO	BS	BA	PTS
L. James	F	46:49	9-24	1-5	8-10	+4	1	10	11	11	1	2	5	3	2	27
K. Love	F	30:02	3-9	0-3	3-4	+19	4	10	14	3	2	2	1	0	0	9
T. Thompson	C	31:49	3-3	0-0	3-4	+2	0	3	3	0	4	0	0	2	0	9
J. Smith	G	38:55	5-13	2-8	0-0	+7	0	4	4	2	3	1	2	0	1	12
K. Irving	G	43:00	10-23	2-5	4-4	+10	3	3	6	1	3	1	2	1	1	26
R. Jefferson		25:30	1-4	0-0	0-0	-8	1	8	9	0	1	1	0	0	1	2
I. Shumpert		19:10	1-3	1-3	3-3	-9	0	1	1	0	0	0	0	0	0	6
M. Williams		04:45	1-3	0-1	0-0	-5	0	0	0	1	0	1	0	0	0	2
M. Dellavedova	DNP - COACH'S DECISION															
C. Frye	DNP - COACH'S DECISION															
D. Jones	DNP - COACH'S DECISION															
J. Jones	DNP - COACH'S DECISION															
T. Mozgov	DNP - COACH'S DECISION															
Total		240	33-82	6-25	21-25		9	39	48	17	15	7	11	6	5	93

TEAM REBS: 11 TOTAL TO: 11

WARRIORS	POS	MIN	FG-A	3P-A	FT-A	+/-	OFF	DEF	TOT	AST	PF	ST	TO	BS	BA	PTS
H. Barnes	F	29:24	3-10	2-4	2-2	-6	0	2	2	1	4	1	0	0	0	10
D. Green	F	46:54	11-15	6-8	4-4	-1	1	14	15	9	3	2	2	0	0	32
F. Ezeli	C	10:45	0-4	0-0	0-0	-9	0	1	1	1	2	0	0	0	2	0
K. Thompson	G	42:17	6-17	2-10	0-0	-11	1	1	2	2	1	3	0	0	14
S. Curry	G	39:16	6-19	4-14	1-1	-3	0	5	5	2	4	1	4	1	1	17
A. Iguodala		37:53	2-6	0-3	0-2	+3	2	7	9	4	3	2	0	2	1	4
A. Varejao		08:29	0-1	0-0	1-2	-9	0	0	0	1	3	0	0	0	1	1
S. Livingston		16:04	3-7	0-0	2-2	+8	1	0	1	2	1	0	1	0	0	8
L. Barbosa		04:24	1-2	1-1	0-0	+5	0	0	0	0	1	0	0	0	1	3
M. Speights		04:34	0-2	0-1	0-0	+3	2	2	4	0	0	0	2	0	0	0
I. Clark	DNP - COACH'S DECISION															
J. McAdoo	DNP - COACH'S DECISION															
B. Rush	DNP - COACH'S DECISION															
Total		240	32-83	15-41	10-13		7	32	39	22	23	7	10	5	6	89

TEAM REBS: 9 TOTAL TO: 10

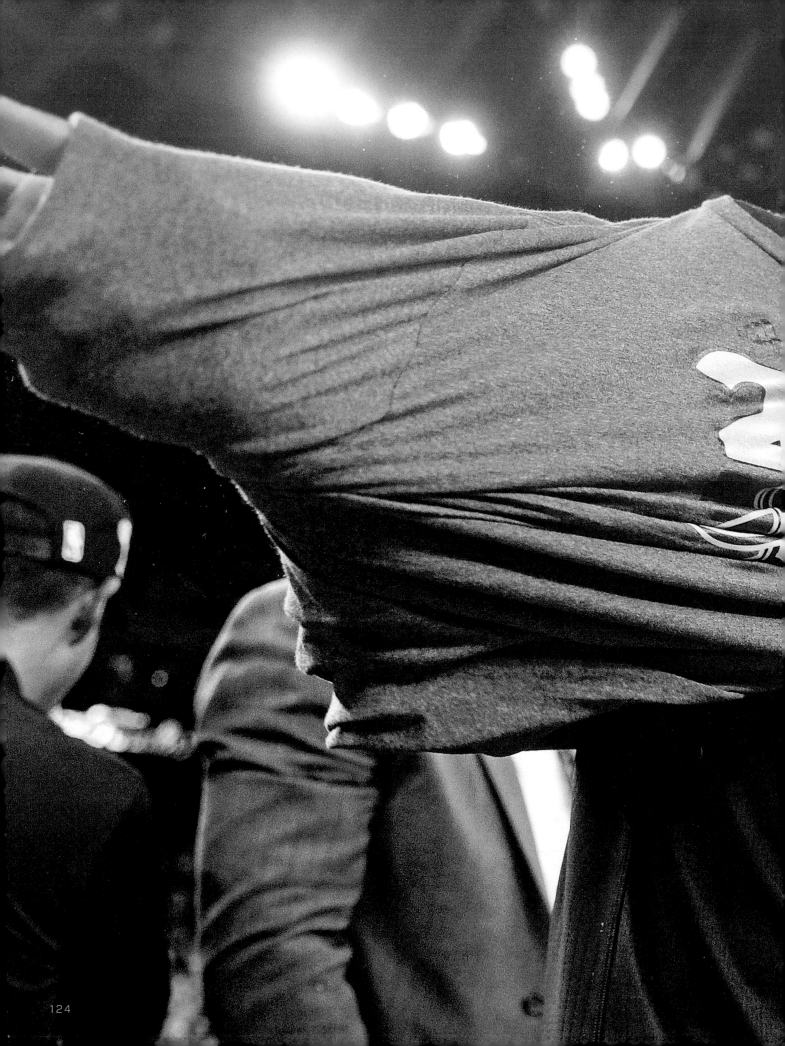

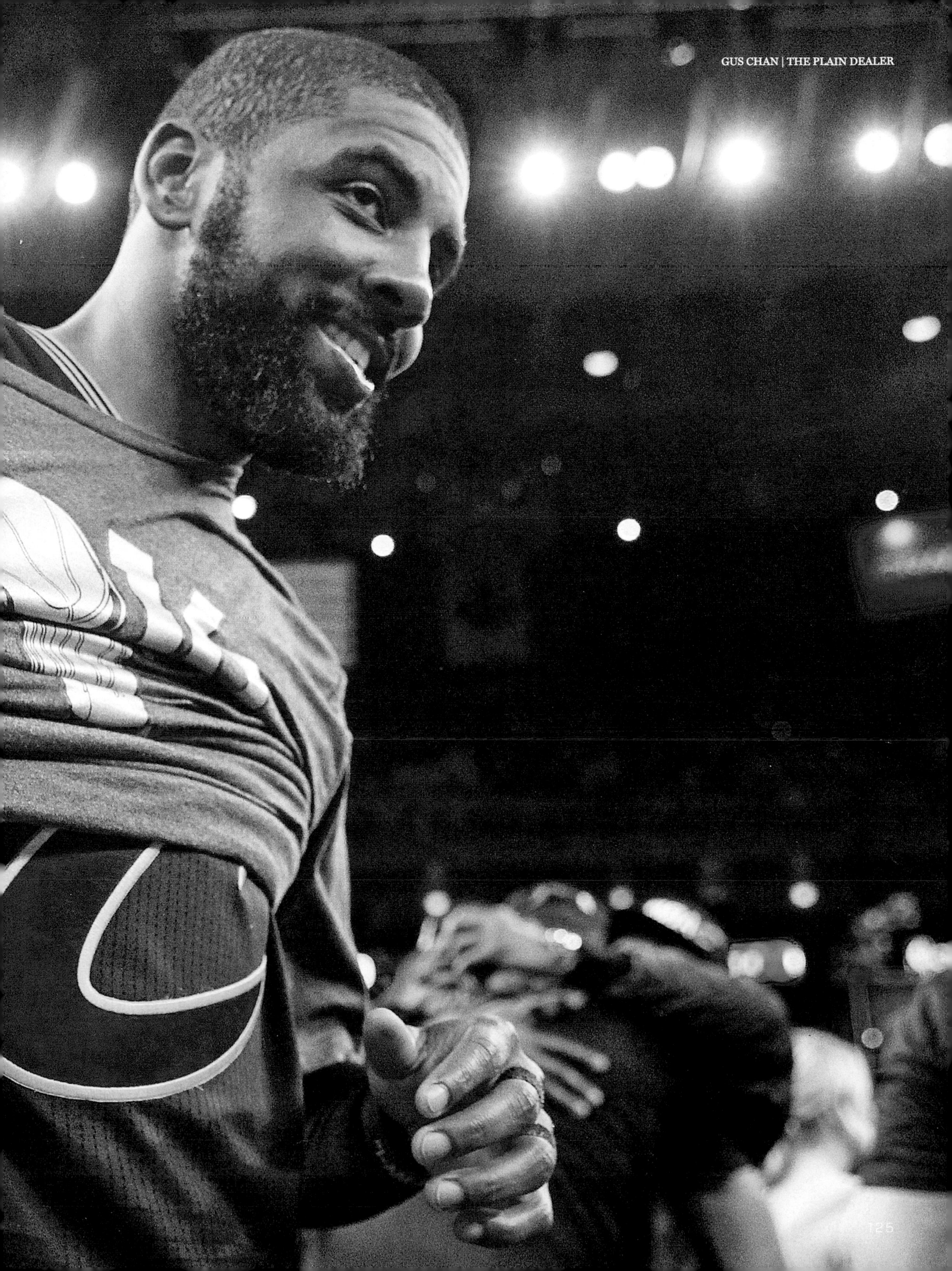
GUS CHAN | THE PLAIN DEALER

Cavaliers fans in downtown Cleveland celebrate the title.

JOSHUA GUNTER
CLEVELAND.COM